Better Homes and Gardens®

handmade

101 GIFT, CAKE & CARD IDEAS FOR AGES 1 TO 101

BIRTHDAYS

Better Homes and Gardens® Books
Des Moines, Iowa

Handmade Birthdays

101 Gift, Cake & Card Ideas for Ages 1 to 101

Better Homes and Gardens® Books
An imprint of Meredith® Books

Editor: Carol Field Dahlstrom
Technical Editor: Susan M. Banker
Graphic Designer: Angie Haupert Hoogensen
Copy Chief: Terri Fredrickson
Copy and Production Editor: Victoria Forlini
Editorial Operations Manager: Karen Schirm
Managers, Book Production: Pam Kvitne,
   Marjorie J. Schenkelberg
Contributing Copy Editor: Arianna McKinney
Contributing Proofreaders: Karen Brewer Grossman,
   Colleen Johnson, Vicki Sidey
Photographers: Andy Lyons Cameraworks,
   Bill Hopkins, Peter Krumhardt, Scott Little
Technical Illustrator: Chris Neubauer Graphics, Inc.
Electronic Production Coordinator: Paula Forest
Editorial and Design Assistants: Kaye Chabot, Mary
   Lee Gavin, Karen McFadden

Meredith® Books
Publisher and Editor in Chief: James D. Blume
Design Director: Matt Strelecki
Managing Editor: Gregory H. Kayko
Executive Editor, Food and Crafts:
   Jennifer Dorland Darling

Director, Operations: George A. Susral
Director, Production: Douglas M. Johnston
Executive Director, Sales: Ken Zagor

Vice President and General Manager:
   Douglas J. Guendel

***Better Homes and Gardens®* Magazine**
Editor in Chief: Karol DeWulf Nickell

Meredith Publishing Group
President, Publishing Group: Stephen M. Lacy
Vice President-Publishing Director: Bob Mate

Meredith Corporation
Chairman and Chief Executive Officer:
   William T. Kerr

Chairman of the Executive Committee:
   E. T. Meredith III

Copyright © 2002 by Meredith Corporation,
Des Moines, Iowa. First Edition.
All rights reserved.
Printed in the United States of America.
Library of Congress Control Number: 2002109228
ISBN: 0-696-21436-9 *(softcover)*
ISBN: 0-696-21535-7 *(hardcover)*

All of us at Better Homes and Gardens® Books are
dedicated to providing you with information and
ideas to create beautiful and useful projects.
We welcome your comments and suggestions.
Write to us at: Better Homes and Gardens Books,
Crafts Editorial Department, 1716 Locust Street—
LN112, Des Moines, IA 50309-3023.

If you would like to purchase any of our crafts,
cooking, gardening, home improvement, or home
decorating and design books, check wherever quality
books are sold. Or visit us at: bhgbooks.com

Cover Photograph: Andy Lyons Cameraworks
   and Scott Little

Our seal assures you that every
recipe in *Handmade Birthdays*
has been tested in the Better
Homes and Gardens® Test Kitchen.
This means that each recipe is
practical and reliable, and meets
our high standards of taste appeal. We guarantee your
satisfaction with this book for as long as you own it.

Happy Birthday!

All of us have one every year. Little ones count the hours until the big day arrives. Teenagers look forward to the day to mark new freedoms. And as adults, some of us lie about how many we have had! Whatever the case, we all love birthdays! Whether turning 6, 16, or 66, a birthday is a special day—a day to mark a point in time, a day to celebrate with the ones you love.

What better way to celebrate a birthday than to surround that special person with handmade treasures— sweet sentiments in the shape of a card, deliciously created and decorated birthday cakes, and handcrafted gifts galore. There is no better way to say, "You're special!" than to present a birthday girl or boy a handmade birthday treat.

So light the candles, sing the birthday song, open the cards and gifts—and have a happy Handmade Birthday!

Carol Field Dahlstrom

How to Use This Book

Happy Greetings!

Get ready to find oodles of inspiration in this book devoted to celebrating birthdays for all ages. You'll bring special meaning to the big day for family and friends as you create wonderful cards, scrumptiously beautiful cakes, and creative gifts.

When making birthday cards—or any greeting cards—you can choose to make the envelope or use a purchased one. We've given you several envelope patterns on pages 62–69. A hint: It's sometimes easier to start with the envelope and then make the card to fit. If necessary, you can adjust the size of any of these cards to fit in a certain envelope, enlarging or decreasing the size of any patterns on a photocopy machine.

When you choose to make a card, you may want to make several of the same design so you can have extras on hand. They will surely be appreciated when it's time to shout, "Happy birthday!"

Happy Baking!

All of the cake, filling, and frosting recipes have been tested in the Better Homes and Gardens® Test Kitchen so you can be assured that they are delicious!

To make baking a breeze, everything you'll need for baking and decorating each cake is listed first on the page. Then the individual ingredients are included with each recipe. If a cake uses a frosting from another recipe, it will be noted for easy reference.

This selection of favorite recipes has risen to new heights with extraordinary new decorating touches. Fondant-topped cakes have always looked elegant, yet may have seemed difficult to make. But now they're easy too (just see pages 74, 88, 102, and 108). For those who enjoy making cut-up cakes, check out the puppy and dinosaur cakes on pages 98 and 100. They're adorable! And if you like cupcakes, don't miss the gumdrop delights on pages 90–95. These pretty mini cakes will please everyone at the party.

Happy Gift Giving!

When choosing a gift to make, you may want to consider how much time you have before beginning. Many of these projects are quick, making them just right for last-minute gifts. Others take a little more time and may require a trip to the crafts store for supplies. To avoid crafting frustration, check the materials list before starting. If any supplies are unusual, you'll find shopping hints listed next to the items.

Then just follow the step-by-step instructions to create a heartfelt birthday gift that is guaranteed to make the day brighter and full of wondrous surprises!

Table of Contents

For more holiday ideas, log onto www.bhg.com/bkholidays

For more cake ideas, visit the Recipe Center at www.bhg.com/bkrecipe

For even more birthday ideas, go to www.bhg.com/bkhomemadebirthday

Cards
pages 6–69

Handmade birthday cards shower the special day with happiness! No matter whose turn it is to celebrate, you'll find the perfect greeting in this chapter. You'll find scrapbook paper ladybugs with beaded antennae, elegant hearts with pearl trim, birthday candles with metallic accents, and many more fun-to-make cards, each one a keepsake destined to be a treasured remembrance of the day.

Cakes
pages 70–113

Birthday cakes are a wonderful tradition that everyone enjoys. Whether you're planning one for a child or an adult, this chapter offers a delicious array of festive cakes that glow with birthday wishes. Hidden beneath a variety of clever decorating techniques, you'll find yummy cake recipes that range from pumpkin spice to white chocolate. And the decorating is pure art! These designs will have party guests singing your praises.

Gifts
pages 114–157

Surprise a dear friend or family member with an unexpected treat—a handmade gift that makes a birthday extra special. Choose from flower-topped tins, seed packet pinwheels, handsome albums, or any of the wonderful gift ideas in this chapter. While some of the projects are so easy that they take just minutes to complete, each one beams with thoughtfulness and creativity.

Cards

Being remembered on your birthday is what truly makes the day special. Forgo the traditional purchased cards and send handmade greetings that shine with love and creativity. You'll find cards in this chapter for all ages and all interests—cards that will surely brighten anyone's day.

Delightful Daisy

Flowers always bring smiles, and this everlasting paper variety
is no exception. Add a glistening gem and a decorative stem to complete
the birthday bloom.

what you'll need

Yellow translucent paper
Papers in white and green
Ruler; pencil
Scissors; crafts knife
Decorative-edge scissors
Kneaded eraser
Glue stick
Tracing paper
Heavy papers in white and green
White glue
Green cord; yellow gem
Green marker
**Purchased envelope or paper, tracing paper,
  and pencil**

here's how

1 This card is made of three folded pieces of
paper and a single yellow panel glued in place
on the inside center panel. Cut an 8¾×8½-inch
piece from yellow, white, and green papers.

2 Score the papers to fold them in half so each
measures 4⅜×8½ inches. To score the papers,
measure and lightly mark with pencil. Hold a ruler
on the fold line and lightly run a knife along edge,
barely breaking the paper surface. Fold each paper
along scored line.

3 On the front panel of green paper, measure in
⅜ inch from the right edge and draw a very
light pencil line. Cut with decorative-edge scissors
along pencil line. On the front panel of white
paper, measure in ⅞ inch from right edge, mark,

and trim with decorative-edge scissors. Measure
1⅛ inches in from the right edge on the yellow
paper, mark, and trim with decorative-edge scissors.
Erase any visible lines with a kneaded eraser.

4 On the back side of the green card, near the
folded edge, run a thin line of glue with glue
stick. Insert the folded green card inside the folded
white card. On the back of the white card, apply
glue and insert into the folded yellow card, lining
up edges at the top and the bottom.

5 Cut a yellow panel to fit inside the center
card. Glue in place.

6 Trace petal/leaf shape, *below,* onto tracing
paper and cut out. Trace shapes onto heavy
white and green papers. Cut out six white petals
and two green leaves.

7 Run a wavy line of white glue onto yellow card.
Apply green cord; glue on white petals and
green leaves. Glue on gem.

PETAL/LEAF
PATTERN

Envelope

1 Use a purchased envelope or use the pattern on
page 62. Enlarge and trace pattern, cut out,
and trace onto desired paper. Cut out with crafts
knife and ruler.

2 To score the fold lines, lightly run a knife along
ruler placed on fold lines, barely breaking the
surface of the paper. Do not apply pressure.

3 Erase any pencil lines with kneaded eraser.

4 Fold in flaps and glue in place with glue stick.

Gift Box Greetings

A birthday is meant for surprises, and this card captures the anticipation.
Scrapbook papers, swirly stickers, and a snippet of ribbon add pretty touches.

what you'll need

Ruler; pencil; lime green paper; scissors
Purple plaid scrapbook paper
Purple swirly and alphabet stickers
Glue stick; crafts knife
½-inch-wide turquoise checkered ribbon
Purchased envelope or paper, tracing paper,
  and pencil

here's how

1 Cut lime green paper to measure 8½×6½ inches. With the short ends together, fold paper in half.

2 Cut a 4×6¼-inch piece of plaid paper. Use a pencil and ruler to measure in ⅜ inch and mark as the inside border. Cut along the markings to make a frame. Cut a 1⅝×2¼-inch rectangle for

the package. Apply swirly stickers randomly to the package.

3 Glue the plaid border centered on the front of the card. Glue the package ¾ inch up from the bottom of the frame, centering left to right.

4 Using a crafts knife, cut ¼-inch-long horizontal slits at the center of the package top and bottom. Cut a 10-inch-long piece of ribbon. Thread the ribbon through the slits, bringing the tails to the right side. Tie a small bow at the package top. Trim the ribbon ends.

5 Adhere the alphabet stickers above the package to spell "it's your day!"

6 Choose a purchased envelope in a coordinating color or see *pages 62–69* for patterns for making envelopes.

Photographic Memories

Use a favorite photo to personalize a birthday greeting. Depending on the photo, you can make the card look silly or stunning or anything in between.

what you'll need

Photograph
Crafts knife
Ruler
Shades of pink paper
Glue stick
Gold writing pen
Birthday cake sticker
White glue
Pink glitter
Purchased envelope or paper,
  tracing paper, and pencil

here's how

1 Crop the photograph as desired using a crafts knife and a ruler. Cut the light pink paper to the desired card size, tearing the short edges.

2 Cut the darker shade of pink paper slightly larger than photo. Tear the edges. Glue the photograph to the dark pink paper. Glue the dark pink paper to the light pink card.

3 Use a gold pen to write messages on light pink paper scraps. Cut out and glue to card.

4 Place a sticker in the lower left corner of the card. Apply white glue along the torn edge of the card front. Sprinkle with glitter. Let the glue dry.

5 Choose a purchased color-coordinated envelope or see *pages 62–69* for patterns for making envelopes. Using white glue, draw a heart shape on the point of the envelope. Sprinkle with glitter. Let dry.

Pamper Yourself

Made from plush scrapbook paper, these miniature slippers are trimmed with button blooms and crafting foam leaves.

what you'll need

Tracing paper; pencil; scissors
Pink velour scrapbook paper
Green crafting foam; needle
Embroidery floss in pink, yellow-orange,
  and turquoise
2 buttons each of yellow and red
3 purple buttons
5¼×10½-inch piece of black paper
White paper; ruler
Glue stick
Thick white crafts glue
Decorative-edge scissors
Black fine-line marker
Paper for envelope
  or purchased
  envelope

here's how

1 Trace the patterns, *opposite,* and cut out the shapes. Trace around sole and leaf patterns on pink velour paper and green foam. Cut out.

2 To create each flower center, thread the needle with embroidery floss. Sew through the button holes three or four times. Knot the floss on the back. Trim the floss ends. One purple button will be used on the inside of the card.

3 Using crafts glue, adhere the inner pink sole to the green foam. Trim ⅛ inch beyond pink. Bend the slipper tops to fit and glue the ends to the sole. Let dry.

4 Glue the button flowers and foam leaves to the slipper tops. Set aside.

5 With the short ends aligning, fold the black paper in half. Measure, mark, and cut thirteen 1-inch squares from white paper. Using a glue stick, adhere the pieces checkerboard-style to the front of the black card. Use crafts glue to hold the slippers in place.

6 For the inside of the card, cut a 4½-inch square from white paper. Glue atop a piece of pink velour paper. Using decorative-edge scissors, trim the pink paper close to the white paper. Glue to the inside of the card. Write "It's Your Birthday... Pamper Yourself!" in the inside of the card. Add a

It's Your Birthday... Pamper Yourself!

button flower and two foam leaves to the lower right-hand corner of the white paper.

7 Choose a purchased color-coordinated envelope or see *pages 62–69* for patterns for making envelopes.

SLIPPER TOP

SLIPPER SOLE

SLIPPER LEAF

You're a Star Card

Pretty enough to frame, this colorful piece of clay will wow anyone. Wrap the card in fancy paper for a giftlike presentation.

what you'll need

Oven-bake clay, such as Sculpey
Rolling pin
Ruler
Star-shape cookie cutter
Items such as beads, buttons, or stamps to make impressions in clay
Black acrylic paint
Small round watercolor paintbrush
Damp cloth
Transparent stains in desired colors (available at stamping and scrapbooking supply stores)
Heavy black paper
Crafts knife; scissors
Velour paper in black and in a desired color
2 patterned papers
Fabrics
⅛-inch-thick crafting foam
Spray adhesive
Copper wire; wire cutters
Beads; white glue
Self-adhesive touch fastener, such as Velcro
14-inch square of paper or fabric for wrap
Ribbon
Gold glitter fabric paint

A

B

here's how

1 Roll out clay to approximately ³⁄₁₆ inch thick. Cut out with a star cookie cutter. Distort star shape, if desired, by gently pulling corners.

2 Make imprints in clay star using desired items as shown in Photo A, *left*.

3 Bake the clay star in the oven according to product instructions. Let cool.

4 Paint the entire star with black acrylic paint. When the paint is nearly dry, use a damp cloth to wipe off the black paint from the most raised areas, leaving it in the crevices. The raised areas should remain fairly white.

5 Using transparent stains, paint the star using small round watercolor brush. Paint the star sections different colors as shown in Photo B. Blend carefully where colors meet. Let dry.

8 Spray the back sides of each piece with spray adhesive. Center the first five layers on the black card from largest to smallest. Next, position the foam in the center and the patterned paper on top of it. The foam will be hidden, as it raises the top layer up a little to give it dimension.

9 Cut two 8-inch-long pieces of copper wire. Curve them and string assorted beads onto them, applying a dab of white glue to the wire ends to hold beads in place. Place beads on wire ends that are visible only. Glue beaded wires onto top panel with white glue. Glue star on top of wires with white glue. Let dry.

10 Apply pieces of self-sticking fastener to back of card and narrow flap if standing card up.

6 From heavy black paper, cut a 7¾×18½-inch piece. Measure, mark, and make score lines as indicated by the diagram on *page 67*. To make a score line, place ruler on fold and run knife gently against ruler, barely breaking the surface of the paper. Fold card at score lines.

7 Cut a 6¾-inch-square panel from velour paper, a 5¾-inch square from one patterned paper, a 5½-inch square from black velour, a 4-inch square of fabric, and a 3¾-inch square of another fabric. Tear a 3-inch square from the other patterned paper. To tear it square, first fold each of the edges to measure 3 inches square; then tear along the folds. Cut a 2-inch square from ⅛-inch-thick crafting foam.

Envelope Wrap

1 Paper or fabric can be used to wrap this card. This wrap was made from a piece of turquoise tissue paper and sheer black fabric. Spray one side of tissue paper with spray adhesive. Apply to back side of sheer fabric.

2 Trim the paper or fabric to a 14-inch square. Wrap card. Tie with a ribbon.

3 Cut two layers of paper and use spray adhesive to attach one to the other. Write "Happy Birthday" on the top layer with gold glitter paint. Let dry.

Golden Petals

In just a couple of easy steps, you can make a floral medallion that will dance in the window of this card. Gold leaf adds a rich glow to the clay.

what you'll need

Oven-bake clay, such as Sculpey
Rubber or clay stamp; glass baking dish
Foil adhesive and brush; gold leafing foil
Textured ivory card stock; ruler; pencil; crafts knife; white glue; kneaded eraser
Purchased envelope or paper, tracing paper, and pencil

here's how

1. Roll a piece of clay into a grape-size ball. Press stamp into the clay until it is approximately ⅛-inch thick as shown in Photo A. Place clay on a baking dish and bake in oven according to product instructions. Let cool.

2. Brush clay piece with foil adhesive. Let dry until tacky. Apply pieces of gold leaf until completely covered as shown in Photo B. Rub foil firmly into crevices.

3. Cut ivory card stock to 11×5 inches. Measure and mark fold lines. To score the fold lines, lay a ruler down and very lightly run knife along edge. Fold in panels.

4. If the card stock has only one good side, cut a piece of paper to fit directly on top of middle panel. Glue in place with glue stick.

5. Cut windows on each end panel. Enlarge the pattern, *right,* or cut irregular squares, making the square on the right end larger.

6. Paint left panel with adhesive. Allow to dry to tacky stage. Apply gold leaf to panel using method in Step 2. Glue clay piece in window.

7. Choose a purchased envelope or see *pages 62–69* for patterns for making envelopes.

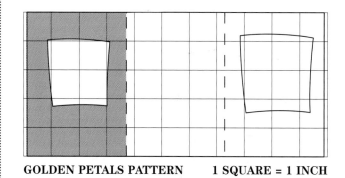

GOLDEN PETALS PATTERN   **1 SQUARE = 1 INCH**

☆Oak Leaf Wishes

A gift from nature makes an elegant statement on the front of this birthday card.

what you'll need
4 coordinating metallic papers (1 textured)
Crafts knife; ruler; pencil
Newspapers
Dried, pressed leaf
Gold spray paint
Spray adhesive
Gold ribbon
White glue; glue stick
Purchased envelope or paper and tracing paper

here's how
1 Cut a 5½×10½-inch piece from textured paper. To score the fold line, lay a ruler on the fold and gently run a crafts knife along the ruler, barely breaking the surface. Fold the card. On the card front, trim ½ inch from the short and bottom edges.

2 From contrasting papers, cut a 2½-inch and a 2¼-inch square for the card front and a 5½-inch square for the inside.

3 In a well-ventilated work area, cover work surface with newspapers. Spray leaf with gold spray paint. Let dry. Spray again if needed. Let dry.

4 Spray adhesive on the back side of the large paper square and adhere it to the inside of the textured panel. Glue the remaining squares in the upper left corner with the smaller square positioned over the larger square.

5 Tie ribbon onto leaf stem. Glue down leaf with small dabs of white glue.

Envelope

1 Use a purchased envelope or the pattern on *page 65*. Enlarge and trace pattern; cut out. Trace around pattern on envelope paper. Cut envelope flap panel and a 2¼-inch and a 2-inch square from coordinating papers as for card.

2 Use glue stick to attach the flap panel and the two layered squares to the envelope flap.

Pretty Pansy Card

No matter the season, flowers send a sentimental message. Add a seed packet to a handmade card and it's a gift come planting time.

what you'll need

Solid paper

Scissors

Seed packet

Thick white crafts glue

Purchased dried flowers

Printed paper; gold writing pen

Paper punch

Narrow satin ribbon

Purchased envelope or paper, tracing paper, and pencil

here's how

1 Cut card to desired size and fold in half. Glue a seed packet on the front of the card.

2 Glue a flower on corner of packet. Cut a piece of printed paper to fit the inside of the card. Write a desired message.

3 Punch hole in edge of the card. Thread ribbon through the hole. Tie into a bow.

4 Choose a purchased, coordinating envelope or see *pages 62–69* for patterns for making envelopes. Glue a dried flower to the flap.

Personalized Chorus

Present the words "Happy Birthday to You" in a classy heart shape
with this pink-on-pink card. Add a paper doily to create a frilly edge.

what you'll need

7¼×11-inch piece of pink floral scrapbook paper
Computer; solid pink paper; tracing paper
Pencil; scissors; glue stick
8-inch square ivory paper doily
7¼×11-inch piece of ivory paper
Pearl trim with flat back
Thick white crafts glue; toothpick
18-inch-long piece of ½-inch-wide pink satin ribbon
18-inch-long piece of 1-inch-wide pink and white
striped satin ribbon
18-inch-long piece of 1½-inch-wide ivory ribbon
Purchased ivory satin roses (available in the
bridal section of crafts and fabric stores)
Purchased envelope or paper

here's how

1 Fold the floral paper in half with the short
ends aligning.

2 Using a computer and a script font, type in the
words to "Happy Birthday to You." If
necessary, adjust the margins so they allow the
type to be at least 7½ inches wide. Repeat the
words until the text is at least 4½ inches high.
Print the text on pink paper.

3 Enlarge and trace the heart pattern, *above
right,* and cut it out. Trace around the
heart pattern on the pink paper. Cut out.

4 Using a glue stick, adhere the centered
heart on one side of the floral paper.

5 Trim one side of the doily to fit
behind the card front. Glue in place.
Fold the ivory paper in half with the short

ends aligning. Glue
it to the inside of
the card.

6 To add the
pearl trim, snip
the strings from one
end. Use a toothpick
to put crafts glue on the back of the first pearl.
Place it at the bottom point of the heart. Continue
gluing the pearls around the heart. Cut the pearl
trim when the center top of the heart is reached.
Repeat for remaining side of heart.

7 Tie ribbons into a bow. Trim ends. Use crafts
glue to adhere bow to upper left corner of
heart. Cut the stems off the satin roses. Glue six or
seven to cover the center of the bow. Let dry.

8 Choose a purchased envelope or see *pages
62–69* for patterns for making envelopes.

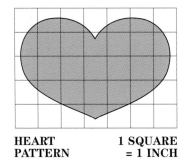

HEART PATTERN   1 SQUARE = 1 INCH

Birthday Cake Card

Here's a clever card for every birthday cake lover! With just a few cuts and a little bit of glue, this festive card is ready to send.

what you'll need

10½×6½-inch piece of black and pink patterned scrapbook paper; 11×8½-inch piece of metallic gold paper, plus a scrap; glue stick

Scallop-edge scissors; tracing paper; pencil

Scissors; patterned scrapbook papers in medium and light pink; round or heart-shape doily

Pink and white birthday candle

Thick white crafts glue

Plastic "Happy Birthday" cupcake trim (available with cake decorating supplies in crafts and discount stores)

Purchased envelope or paper

here's how

1. Fold the black and pink patterned paper in half with the short ends together. Fold one piece of gold paper in half with short ends together. Use a glue stick to adhere patterned paper over gold. Use scallop-edge scissors to trim edge of gold paper close to patterned paper.

2. Trace the pattern pieces, *right*. Cut out. Trace around the frosting and filling patterns on the light pink patterned paper, and the cake patterns on the medium pink patterned paper. Cut out.

3. Cut a small section of doily to fit the bottom of card. Glue in place. Glue cake pieces over doily. For the trim around the candle, cut a round section from the remaining piece of doily. Cut off the bottom of the candle so it measures 1½ inches.

If needed, cut a slit in the center of the doily piece and slide candle through.

4. Glue the candle in place on the cake using thick white crafts glue.

5. Cut a quarter-size circle from gold paper, reversing the scallop scissors to create a wavy effect. Glue behind the candle wick. Use crafts glue to adhere the plastic cupcake trim in place.

6. Choose a purchased envelope or see *pages 62–69* for patterns for making envelopes.

CAKE PATTERN

Seashell Sentiments

Wish someone special a day as calming as the waves against the shore with this seashell card, complete with hand-painted watercolor paper.

what you'll need

Heavy watercolor paper
Water and paintbrush
Watercolor paint in teal blue and coral
Salt
Pencil; ruler
Crafts knife
⅛-inch-thick white crafting foam
Scissors
Decoupage medium
White glitter
White glue
Seashells
Gold pen
Purchased envelope or paper, tracing paper, iridescent paper, kneaded eraser, and glue stick

here's how

1 Soak watercolor paper front and back with water. Lay flat onto surface. Dip brush into teal blue paint and dot onto wet surface, allowing paint to bleed into water as shown in Photo A, *left*. Before paint dries sprinkle salt onto surface as shown in Photo B. Let dry. Shake off excess salt.

2 Trim the painted paper to measure 8⅝×4½ inches. To make the fold, measure 4½ inches from the end and mark the fold line. Score the fold line by running a knife lightly along pencil line. Avoid cutting through paper. Fold painted side outward so the front panel is shorter than the back panel.

Envelope

1 Use a purchased envelope or use the pattern on *page 69.* Enlarge and trace the pattern onto tracing paper; cut out. Trace around the envelope pattern on the envelope paper and the shell patterns on iridescent paper. Cut out with crafts knife and ruler.

2 To score the fold lines, lightly run the knife along ruler placed on fold lines, barely breaking the surface of the paper. Do not apply pressure.

3 Erase any pencil lines with kneaded eraser.

4 Glue shell paper pieces onto the flap using a glue stick. Fold in flaps and glue in place.

3 Paint the bottom of the inside panel with water. When paper is well-saturated, paint a coral color onto wet paper, allowing paint to bleed into water. Sprinkle with salt and allow to dry. Shake off excess salt.

4 Enlarge and trace wavy pattern, *right.* Cut out. Trace around pattern on white crafting foam. Cut out. Trim sides to fit onto card.

5 Paint a heavy coat of decoupage medium. Sprinkle with white glitter as shown in Photo C, *opposite.* Let dry.

6 Adhere shells in place using white glue. Let dry.

7 Glue glittered piece to card. Write "Happy Birthday" below glittered piece.

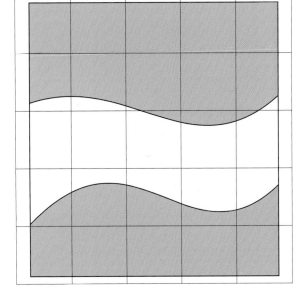

SHELL CARD PATTERN   1 SQUARE = 1 INCH

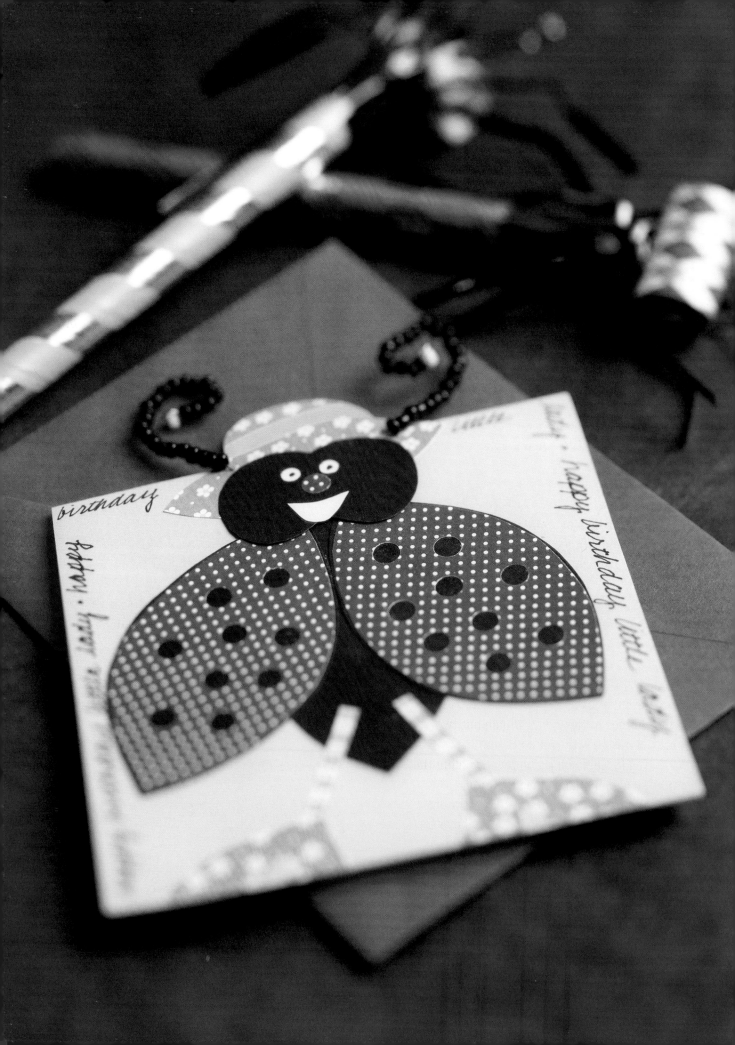

Lucky Ladybug Card

All dressed up for a party, this birthday bug will deliver greetings to any little friend. Colorful scrapbook papers add details to the ladybug.

what you'll need

Tracing paper; pencil
Scissors
Printed scrapbook papers in red, turquoise, and green
Solid papers in black, white, and orange
5×10-inch piece of yellow card stock
Paper punch; glue stick
Wire; wire cutters
Ruler; straight pin
Large seed beads in black and white
Black fine-line marking pen
Purchased envelope or paper

here's how

1 Trace the patterns on *page 29*. Cut out patterns and trace around shapes on the corresponding color of paper. Cut out the pieces.

2 With right sides together, align the ladybug's red wings. Use a paper punch to make symmetrical holes in the wings. Punch out two white eyes.

3 Referring to the diagram on *page 28,* glue the paper shapes in place on yellow card.

4 Cut a 6-inch piece of wire. Using a straight pin, poke two holes in the hat just above the ladybug's face. Feed the wire through the holes. Thread 22 black beads and one white bead onto each wire end as shown, *right*. Push each wire end back through two or three black beads to secure. Trim the excess wire.

5 Use a black marking pen to write "happy birthday little lady" around the top and side edges of the card. Add a black dot to the center of each eye.

6 Choose a purchased, coordinating envelope or see *pages 62–69* for patterns for making envelopes.

BEADING DIAGRAM

LADYBUG ASSEMBLY DIAGRAM

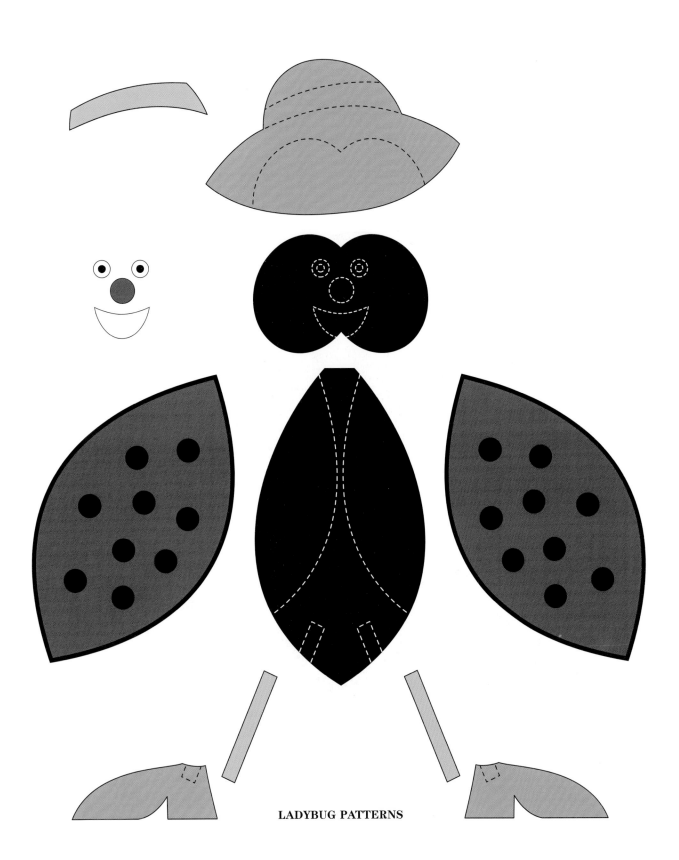

LADYBUG PATTERNS

Perky in Pastel

Spell out birthday wishes that sparkle with sincerity. White glittered letters dance on pretty pastel papers for this jubilant greeting.

what you'll need

Pastel patterned card stock; ruler; crafts knife
Small pieces of pastel papers; waxed paper
Decoupage medium; paintbrush; white glitter
Scissors; white dimensional fabric paint
Clear acetate (available in art stores)
Clear tape; spray adhesive; glue stick
Purchased envelope or 2 colors of
    envelope paper

here's how

1 Cut the pastel patterned card stock to measure 4½×8½ inches. To make a card, fold the paper with the short ends together. Place assorted pastel papers on waxed paper. Spread a thin coat of decoupage medium onto each piece of paper and sprinkle with white glitter as shown in Photo A, *right.* Let dry.

2 Cut 14 varying squares and rectangles from glittered paper with sides ranging from ½ inch to 1½ inches. Arrange pastel paper pieces on the card front as background pieces to spell "Happy Birthday!"

3 Carefully remove the pieces from the card, keeping the arrangement intact. Glue the overlapping pieces together. Let dry.

4 Draw a letter on each block and outline each block with white dimensional paint as shown in Photo B. Sprinkle with glitter. Let dry.

5 Cut a piece of clear acetate the same size as the card front. Place the card facedown on a flat work surface. Lay the acetate piece alongside card, butting the edges together. Tape the pieces together using one strip of clear tape from top to bottom. Trim off excess tape.

6 In a well-ventilated work area, spray adhesive on the back of the blocks and attach them to the acetate.

7 Choose a purchased, coordinating envelope or see *pages 62–69* for patterns for making envelopes. Line the envelope, if desired, with a contrasting color of paper.

Make-a-Wish Card

The beloved tradition of blowing out birthday candles shines through on this reversible fold-up card. Add a single candle to the envelope for a bonus wish.

what you'll need
2 colored papers
Spray adhesive; ruler; pencil
Scissors; crafts knife
Tube-style fabric paint
Adhesive-back metallic orange paper
Paperback adhesive tabs (found with scrapbooking and photo supplies)
Tracing paper; purchased envelope or paper

here's how

1 This card can be displayed standing or in a ring with ends taped together. To determine the length of the card, decide on the number of 1-inch-wide candles you need. To secure the card in a ring, you must end up with an odd number of panels. The end panels will overlap each other and connect.

2 Spray adhesive to the back side of one paper. Attach to the back of the remaining colored paper, aligning the bottom edges.

3 Cut the rectangular piece to measure 2¾ inches high and the desired length.

4 With the rectangular strip lying horizontally, measure in 2 inches from the left side and mark every 2 inches the entire length of the card.

5 Make a vertical score line at each 2-inch mark by placing a ruler by the marks and gently running a knife along the edge, barely breaking the surface of the paper.

6 Turn the paper over and repeat the same process, making the first score 2 inches from the left side so that score lines alternate every 1 inch on the front and back.

7 Measure according to pattern, *opposite,* and cut

the top angles of the candles.

8 Use fabric paint to write "Happy Birthday." Use one or more letters per candle or stack the words. Let dry and repeat on the other side.

9 Trace flame pattern, *left,* onto tracing paper, cut out, and trace onto metallic orange twice for each candle. Cut out, remove backing, and apply to candles.

10 Apply adhesive tabs on end candle, leaving on the paper backing. The recipient can remove the backing and arrange to secure the card in a ring if desired.

11 Choose a purchased, coordinating envelope or see *pages 62–69* for patterns for making envelopes.

FLAME PATTERN

Die-Cut Card

Embossed paper, readily available at scrapbooking stores,
makes creating this heavenly hello a cinch.

what you'll need

Ruler; scissors; green paper; ivory embossed paper
Pencil; crafts knife; glue stick
Adhesive-backed touch fastener, such as Velcro
Purchased envelope or paper; kneaded eraser

here's how

1 Cut a 5½-inch square from green paper. Trim
ivory embossed paper to 5½×11½ inches.

2 Measure in 3 inches from each end and draw a
fold line on outside of ivory card. To score
each fold line, lay down ruler and gently run knife
along ruler, barely breaking the surface of the
paper. Fold the paper with scores facing outward.

3 Using the pattern of the paper as a guide, trim
each side to an interesting shape. Make sure
to leave an area where the panels overlap.

4 Glue green paper in the center of ivory paper.
Apply touch fastener where the panels overlap.

Envelope

1 Use a purchased envelope or use the pattern on
page 66. Enlarge and trace the pattern; cut out.
Trace around pattern on envelope paper. Cut out.

2 To score fold lines, lightly run the knife along
ruler placed on fold lines, barely breaking the
surface. Erase pencil lines with a kneaded eraser.

3 Fold in flaps and hold in place with sticker.
Cut two pieces of the card paper, layer one on
top of the other, and glue in place. Write "Happy
Birthday" on the top tag. Use touch fastener to
attach the tag over the envelope flap.

Stamped Salutations

The popular art of rubber stamping makes kids' play out of this classy card. While this card is covered with a leaf pattern, you can use any stamp design you like to add pizzazz to your handmade birthday cards.

what you'll need
Black glossy card stock
Ruler; crafts knife
Colored paper
Stamp and black ink pad
Black fabric paint; black marker
Glue stick; green cord
Purchased envelope or paper, tracing paper, and pencil

here's how

1 Cut the black paper to measure 5×8 inches. Measure to find the center fold line. To score the card, lay ruler along fold line and lightly run knife along edge of ruler without cutting through the paper. Fold along score line.

2 Trim a piece of colored paper to fit front panel. To leave the blank space for words in the middle of the card, lay down a piece of paper there and stamp design; then remove paper.

3 Write "Happy Birthday" with black fabric paint. Let dry.

4 Use a black marker to draw a curvy edge to separate the stamping from the "Happy Birthday." Glue stamped paper onto black card. Tie a green cord around the folded edge.

5 Choose a purchased, coordinating envelope or see *pages 62–69* for patterns for making envelopes.

Happy Birdy

This silly character will bring a smile to the face of any birthday boy or girl. The wispy black feather and a combination of velour paper and card stock provide fun textures.

what you'll need
Tracing paper; pencil; scissors
Blue velour paper
Card stock in orange, red, and white
Newspapers
Spray adhesive; crafts knife; ruler
Glue stick
Black marker; black tube-style fabric paint
Black feather
Tape
Purchased envelope or paper and
    kneaded eraser

here's how
1 Trace the patterns for the bird onto tracing paper. Cut out patterns. Trace around the patterns on the corresponding papers.

2 In a well-ventilated work area, cover the work surface with newspapers. For the top orange beak, spray the back side of the orange paper with spray adhesive. Press the orange beak piece onto a piece of red paper. Trim excess red paper, cutting along the orange beak shape.

3 On the orange side of the beak, use a crafts knife to score the line indicated on pattern.

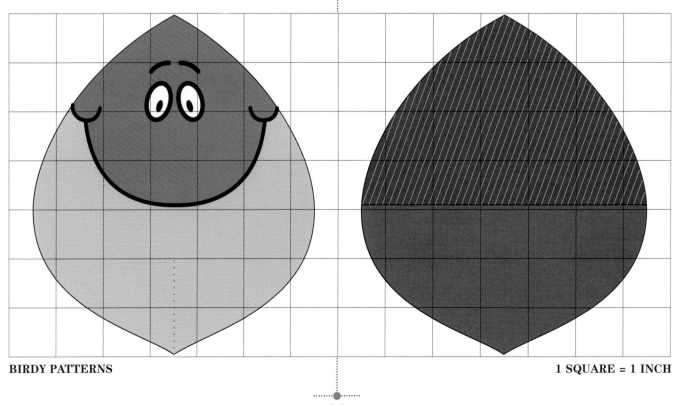

BIRDY PATTERNS

1 SQUARE = 1 INCH

To make a score line, hold a ruler down and lightly run a crafts knife along the edge without cutting through. Fold in gently to shape beak.

4 Refer to the striped glue area on pattern and glue the beak onto the red base piece, lining up edges. Glue the blue velour paper in place.

5 Using a black marker, draw around the white eyes and add black pupils. Cut out the eyes and glue in place on the blue velour.

6 Using black paint, outline the blue area, draw eyebrows and write "Happy Birdy." Keep the card open until dry.

7 Tape a black feather to the back of the card.

Envelope

1 Choose a purchased envelope or use the pattern on *page 64*. Enlarge and trace the pattern; cut out. Trace around the pattern on envelope paper. Cut out with crafts knife and ruler.

2 To score the fold lines, lightly run a knife along ruler placed on fold lines, barely breaking the surface of the paper. Erase any pencil lines using a kneaded eraser.

3 Fold in the flaps and use a glue stick to adhere in place.

Colorful Foiled Greeting

Metallic foils shimmer against a black paper background, making
this card a real attention getter. This card includes a freehand candle design,
but you can incorporate any simple motif.

what you'll need

Black card stock
Pencil
Ruler
Crafts knife or paper cutter
Foil adhesive
Colored foils
Ribbon or cord
Black paper for envelope
Foil paper
Spray adhesive
Glue stick
**Purchased envelope or black and foil papers and
    tracing paper**

here's how

1 Cut the black card stock to measure
9×7¾ inches.

2 Using a pencil, measure and lightly mark the
fold line in the center so when folded the card
measures 4½ inches wide.

3 To score the fold line along marked pencil
line, lightly run knife along pencil line just
enough to break the paper surface. Fold the card
with scored line to the outside.

4 Pencil in the letters and candles. Draw them
in your own style or use this card for
inspiration. Draw over the pencil lines with
adhesive. Allow to dry until tacky.

5 Do one section at a time. Press foil onto
adhesive according to instructions with the
shiny side up. Remove the foil from adhesive,
leaving the color on the card. Repeat until the card
is covered.

6 Tie a ribbon or cord around the fold of card.
Tie the ends into a bow. Trim the ends.

Envelope

1 Use a purchased envelope or use a pattern from
pages 62–69. Enlarge and trace the envelope
pattern; cut out. Trace around the pattern on black
paper. Cut out envelope.

2 Cut out a piece of colored foil paper for the
inside of the envelope. Apply spray adhesive to
the back side of the paper. Attach the foil color to
the inside of black paper, lining up the corners of
the envelope. Trim the foil paper to match the
black paper envelope flap.

3 Score fold lines. Lightly run the crafts knife
along fold lines, barely breaking the surface of
the paper. Fold in sections with scored lines on the
outside. Glue the flaps in place with a glue stick.

Artful Message

The variety of materials on this keepsake card lend a wonderful blend of texture and color.

what you'll need

Canvas; stamp and large black ink pad
Spray adhesive; ¼-inch-thick black crafting foam
Ruler; pencil; scissors; water-based stains
Card stock and 2 contrasting papers
3 different coordinating decorative yarns
  (available in scrapbooking and paper stores)
White glue; crafts knife; straight pins
Scrap of ⅛-inch-thick black crafting foam; pens
  in black and gold; seed beads; tissue paper
Card stock for wrap

here's how

1 Using black ink, stamp a design onto canvas as shown in Photo A, *left*. Let dry.

2 Spray a heavy coat of adhesive on the back side of the canvas. Apply to ¼-inch-thick black foam. Press firmly.

3 Draw a square penciled line approximately 4×3½ inches. Use scissors to trim the piece of canvas along the pencil lines.

4 Paint desired colors of stains, such as blue, red, and gold to cover stamped canvas. Blend colors with paintbrush as shown in Photo B. Let dry.

5 Trim card stock to 10×7 inches. Mark fold line with pencil so it folds to 5×7 inches. Score along fold line. Hold a ruler along edge and run knife lightly along edge to barely break surface of paper. Fold the card with score line outside.

6 Trim contrasting paper to about 3×8 inches. Spray back side with spray adhesive and apply vertically centered to card. Use knife and ruler to trim off excess paper on top and bottom.

7 Place a small amount of white glue along the edges and in the center of the contrasting panel. Wrap yarn on edges of panel to make a border. Wrap another yarn over center panel randomly, allowing some of the paper to show through as shown in Photo C.

8 Spread glue on back side of canvas piece and position onto card. Place glue around edge of foam. Wrap yarn around and pin in place until dry.

9 Adhere another piece of contrasting paper onto the thin foam. Trim to measure 2½×¾ inches. Write "Happy Birthday" with black pen and trace over the black with a gold pen. Glue with white glue onto center of stamped piece. Outline piece with a strand of seed beads, gluing in place.

Envelope Wrap

1 Spray one side of card stock with spray adhesive. Allow to dry to tacky stage. Apply tissue paper and smooth out wrinkles.

2 Trim piece to 13¾×7¾ inches (pattern on *page 68*). Use a ruler and pencil to mark fold lines. Score on fold lines. Lay down ruler and lightly run knife along edge, barely breaking surface. Remember that the side of paper that you score on will fold outward. Cut edge of short flap using pinking shears.

3 Cut tiny slits in fold through which to insert yarn. Wrap card, fold wrapping, and tie with yarn.

Celebration Card

Perfect for a little one's birthday, this foam card announces an important year.

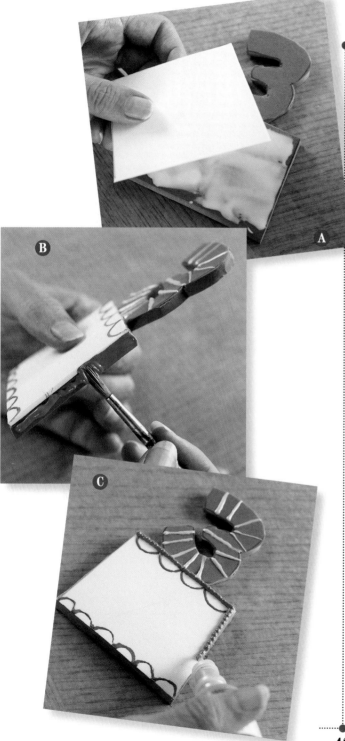

what you'll need
Tracing paper; pencil
Scissors; ¼-inch-thick colored crafting foam
⅛-inch-thick white crafting foam
Tape; thick white crafts glue; paintbrush
Tube-style fabric paint in desired colors
Decorative-edge scissors
Purchased envelope or paper and glue stick

here's how
1 Create your own pattern by combining the cake pattern, *below,* and whichever number(s) needed, *opposite.* Trace patterns onto tracing paper, cut out, tape together, and trace onto a piece of thick foam. Trace cake piece onto white foam. Cut out pieces with scissors.

2 Spread crafts glue on front of cake section of colored foam base. Align and glue white foam on base as shown in Photo A, *left.*

3 Paint the sides of the foam as shown in Photo B. Decorate the cake and number(s) using

3

Happy
Birthday!

**CAKE
PATTERN**

**1 SQUARE
= 1 INCH**

fabric paints as shown in Photo C. Let dry.

4 Choose a purchased, coordinating envelope or see *pages 62–69* for patterns for making envelopes. Use decorative-edge scissors to cut a contrasting paper strip and glue on the envelope flap.

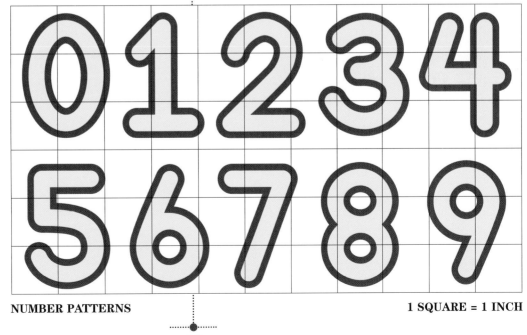

NUMBER PATTERNS

1 SQUARE = 1 INCH

Pressed Posies Card

Keep pressed pretties on hand year-round to make blooming birthday greetings.

what you'll need

Heavy card stock; crafts knife; ruler
⅛-inch-thick white crafting foam; spray adhesive
Pressed flowers; paintbrush; decoupage medium
Solid-colored paper; patterned pastel paper
Purchased envelope or paper, tracing paper,
 pencil, and glue stick

here's how

1. Cut heavy card stock to measure 3½×4 inches for the flower background and 10×5½ inches for card. Fold the background piece in half. Trim a piece of foam to 3½×4 inches.

2. Spray one side of foam with adhesive and apply to the same size card stock.

3. Arrange flowers on card and brush on decoupage medium as flowers are placed on paper. When all flowers are arranged, brush one final coat of decoupage medium over surface. Reserve some flowers for envelope.

4. Cut a piece of contrasting paper larger than the inside panel of card. Spray the back side with adhesive. Apply to inside panel, lining up straight edge of colored paper at the fold. Trim off excess paper with a crafts knife.

5. Repeat the same process for the front card panel using a different coordinating paper.

6. On the front panel, measure in ⅝ inch from each edge, drawing a light pencil line. Open the card and cut out window using a crafts knife.

7. Close front panel, apply spray adhesive to back of foam, and affix centered in place through the window onto the inside panel.

Envelope

1. Choose a purchased, coordinating envelope or see *pages 62–69* for patterns for making envelopes.

2. Glue a pressed flower on the envelope flap using the same process as on the card.

Beaded Birthday Card

Tiny seed beads parade around a window of decorative paper as the focal point of this birthday greeting. Press-on lettering completes the good wishes.

what you'll need
2 coordinating printed papers
Scissors; ruler; decorative-edge scissors
White rice paper; glue stick; seed beads
Thread; beading needle; thick white crafts glue
Alphabet stickers; purchased envelope or paper,
  tracing paper, and pencil

here's how
1 Cut card paper to measure 10×6½ inches. Fold the paper in half with the short ends together. Trim one short end with decorative-edge scissors.

2 Cut a 5×8½-inch piece of rice paper. Fold in half with short ends together. Place over folded card, folds together. Glue in place.

3 Cut a 6½×1-inch strip from coordinating paper. Glue to right-hand edge of inside panel. Cut a 1⅛×1¼-inch piece from coordinating paper. Glue to a scrap from background color paper. Trim ⅛ inch beyond coordinating paper. Glue onto rice paper. Trim ¼ inch beyond edge of background color paper. Glue to center of card front.

4 Thread needle. Thread seed beads on thread to a length that fits around the colored papers in the center of the card. Tie the thread ends together. Use crafts glue to adhere the beads in place. Let dry. Use stickers to spell Happy Birthday.

5 Choose a purchased, coordinating envelope or see *pages 62–69* for patterns for making envelopes.

Sticker Cards

With all the stickers available today, you'll have no trouble
finding just the right theme for a birthday card. Keep an assortment in your
crafting drawer to make last-minute cards.

what you'll need

Patterned or plain scrapbook papers
Scissors; paper punch
Rubber stamps and ink pads
Marking pens
Ribbon
Glue stick
Stickers
Spacers, such as Pop Dots, in desired
  thicknesses

here's how

1 Cut the background paper(s) to the desired
size. Fold the card in half if desired.

2 To add punched-out shapes, such as circles
or stars, to any of the paper layers, use a
paper punch and make the designs as desired.

3 To stamp any of the papers, press the
rubber stamp on the ink pad and
press onto the paper. Draw designs
with markers if desired.

4 To thread a ribbon through the paper, punch
holes or cut slits where desired. Thread the
ribbon through the openings. Tie a bow with the
ribbon ends if desired.

5 Glue any paper layers in place. Add stickers or
stamped paper pieces where desired. To raise
paper pieces, add a spacer, such as Pop Dots.

6 Choose a purchased, coordinating
envelope or see *pages 62–69* for patterns
for making envelopes.

what you'll need

**Crafts knife; 3 coordinating papers
Ruler; pencil; glue stick; cinnamon stick
Dried leaf; thick white crafts glue; raffia
Purchased envelope or paper, tracing paper,
scissors, and an acorn cap**

here's how

1. Use a crafts knife to cut a 4½×11-inch card from desired background paper.

2. To score the card where it will fold, place a ruler in the center of the card. Lightly run a knife across the fold line, barely breaking surface of paper. Fold the paper.

3. Tear next layer of paper to measure approximately 3×5½ inches. To make tearing easier, fold it to this dimension first and then tear. Apply glue stick to the back side and affix to card, folding the edge over the top.

4. Tear the top paper to measure 2¼×3¾ inches. Use glue stick to attach the paper to the card, allowing room to write on bottom. Write happy birthday at lower edge of middle paper.

5. Use a small amount of white glue to attach cinnamon stick and leaf. Let dry.

6. Tie raffia around the top fold.

Envelope

1. Use a purchased envelope or use the pattern on *page 64*. Enlarge and trace the pattern; cut out. Trace around the pattern on envelope paper. Cut out. Score the fold lines as indicated. Use glue stick to assemble the envelope.

2. Apply a generous dab of crafts glue to an acorn cap and apply to envelope below flap. Let dry.

3. Insert card. Tie raffia around envelope and around acorn.

Nature enthusiasts will love this card. Raffia and a dried leaf accent the candle.

Cinnamon Stick Card

Big-Win Note

Play money adds a wishful touch to this easy-to-make birthday card.
Computer-generated type gives the card a professional look.

what you'll need

Patterned green paper
Play money, such as Monopoly money
Glue stick
Computer-generated lettering
White paper
Scissors
Pinking shears
Solid-color coordinating paper

here's how

1 Fold card to desired size. Glue money to the front of card as desired.

2 Use a computer to type "Hope you Win Big on your BIRTHDAY!" on white paper. Trim close to the lettering, pinking the top edge. Glue to solid-colored paper. With lettering at the top, cut a 2¾-inch-wide strip from solid-color paper and glue to inside edge of the card.

3 Choose a purchased, coordinating envelope or see *pages 62–69* for patterns for making envelopes.

Blooming Buttons

Floral buttons are available in a variety of styles. Pick a bloom to match the personality of your birthday buddy and make this clever card as quick as a wink.

what you'll need

Papers in red, yellow, and green
Spray adhesive
Scissors
Ruler and crafts knife
White textured paper
White glue
Button
Wire cutters
Fabric paint in green
and red
Paper punch

here's how

1. In a well-ventilated work area, spray back side of red paper with adhesive. Lay the yellow paper onto the adhesive and smooth with hands. Trim the layered papers to measure 5½×8½ inches.

2. Use a ruler to measure the center of the paper and lightly mark. To score the fold, lightly run a knife along the edge of ruler. Fold the paper so the red is on the outside.

3. Cut a piece of textured paper to fit the front panel of the card. Glue it in place with white glue.

4. Clip off back of button with wire cutters. Glue it onto the white panel.

5. Draw lines in with green fabric paint. Let dry.

6. Cut a piece of green paper and write "Happy Birthday" in red. Let dry. Glue onto white panel. Use a paper punch to make random holes in red paper.

7. Choose a purchased, coordinating envelope or see *pages 62–69* for patterns for making envelopes.

Party Hats Card

Miniature party hats lend festive flair to a stamped card and accompanying bookmark.

what you'll need

Precut scalloped postcards
Paper punch
Colored marking pens, glitter pens, and/or gel pens
Round spacers, such as Pop Dots
Scrapbook paper in assorted solid colors and prints
Decorative-edge scissors
Small rubber stamp and ink pad
Party hat and alphabet stickers
¼-inch-wide sheer ribbon
Precut bookmarks

here's how

1 For card, punch holes around the edge of a scalloped postcard. Add a freehand design around the edge using a colored pen.

2 Using spacers, attach the postcard to a piece of printed scrapbook paper. Trim just beyond postcard using decorative-edge scissors.

3 For the top layer, fold a piece of paper in half. Using decorative-edge scissors, cut the card slightly smaller than postcard without cutting the folded edge. Stamp the front as desired and add hat stickers. Use spacers to attach the top folded card layer to the postcard. Add a ribbon to the top of the card by threading it through two holes in the scalloped border of the postcard.

4 To make a bookmark, cut a strip from scrapbook paper. Add hat and alphabet stickers. Use a paper punch to add polka-dot holes between the stickers as desired. Thread ribbon through two holes on one end of the bookmark. Tie the ribbon into a bow.

5 Choose a purchased, coordinating envelope or see *pages 62–69* for patterns for making envelopes.

Serene Sentiments

Backyard snippets and paint create this trees-and-birds scene perfect for the nature enthusiast. Dusted with gold, the card is a reflection of the glorious outdoors.

what you'll need

Cardboard, textured illustration, or mat board
Ruler; pencil; crafts knife; decoupage medium
Evergreen or any dry fernlike green; paintbrush
Tube-style fabric paint; burgundy acrylic paint
Gold highlighting, such as Rub 'n Buff
Gold card stock; burgundy velour paper
Spray adhesive; white glue; glue stick
Purchased envelope or paper and tracing paper

A

B

here's how

1. Trim cardboard to measure 3¾×4¾ inches. Arrange pressed evergreen on cardboard. Place in a heavy book overnight to press flat.

2. Paint geese (elongated Ms) in sky and "Happy Birthday" using fabric paint. Let dry.

3. Brush decoupage medium on card and on evergreen as shown in Photo A, *right*. Let dry.

4. Paint over entire surface with burgundy paint. Let dry.

5. Using very little gold highlighting, gently apply over raised surfaces using fingertip as shown in Photo B. Apply several thin layers.

6. Trim the gold card stock to 4⅛×5⅛ inches. Trim the velour paper to 9¼×5⅝ inches. Fold burgundy paper in half. If the back side of card needs reinforcing, apply a piece of gold card stock cut to 4⅝×5⅝ inches. Spray back side of gold piece with adhesive and attach to inside of back panel.

7. Spread a thin layer of white glue on back side of gold card stock and apply centered onto front of card. Apply glue on burgundy painted piece and apply centered on top of gold piece.

Envelope

1. Use a purchased envelope or use the pattern on *page 68*. Enlarge and trace the pattern; cut out. Trace around the pattern on paper. Cut out.

2. Score the fold lines. Lightly run the knife along ruler placed on fold lines, barely breaking the surface. Erase any pencil lines. Fold in flaps and glue in place with glue stick.

Lovely Lavender Card

Lavender and gold are a striking combination for this easy-to-do cut-and-glue card.

what you'll need

3 coordinating papers in solid lavender, solid gold, and patterned gold and lavender
Gold pen; pencil; ruler; crafts knife
Spray adhesive; narrow gold braid trim; scissors
White glue; kneaded eraser; glue stick
Purchased envelope or paper and tracing paper

here's how

1 Cut lavender paper to measure 5½×11 inches. To score center fold line, measure and mark the center of card. Lay down a ruler and very lightly run knife along ruler just enough to barely break the surface of the paper.

2 Fold card with score line outward. Cut patterned paper into a 3½-inch square. Spray back side with spray adhesive and attach to front of card.

3 Cut another 1½-inch lavender square, apply spray adhesive, and attach to center of card.

4 Write "Happy Birthday" using golden pen. Draw a fine line of white glue around edges of papers and apply golden braid.

Envelope

1 Use a purchased envelope or use the patterns on *page 58*. Enlarge and trace the patterns; cut out. Trace around envelope on gold paper. Cut out with crafts knife. Cut a lavender liner piece larger than pattern.

2 Spray back side of lavender liner with adhesive. Affix to inside of gold panel. Trim to match gold paper.

3 Cut the two lavender panels, spray the back side with adhesive, and attach to panels.

4 To score fold lines, lay down ruler on fold lines and lightly run knife along edge, barely breaking the surface. Fold panels outward.

5 Run a thin line of white glue along panels and apply gold braid trim. Fold in panels and seal with glue stick.

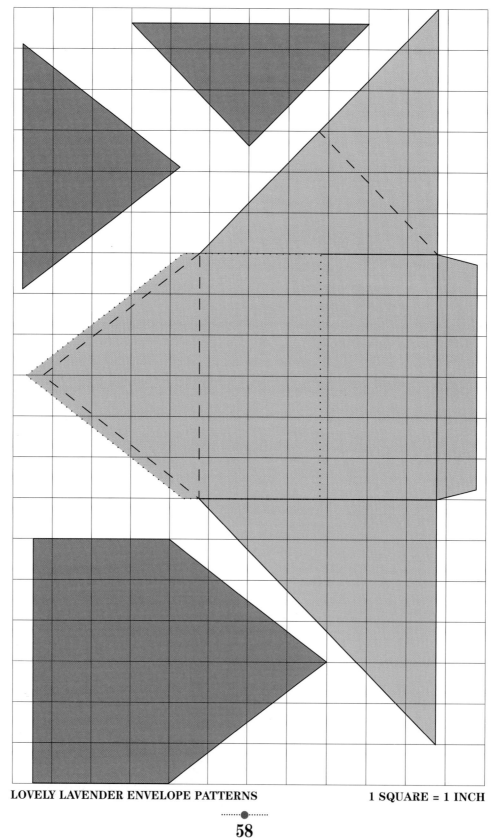

LOVELY LAVENDER ENVELOPE PATTERNS   **1 SQUARE = 1 INCH**

Window Card

Here's a card with a view that brings a touch of sunshine to the birthday celebrator. Colorful bead trim creates a sparkling curtain edge for this creative birthday card.

what you'll need

Pink velour scrapbook paper; scissors
Ruler; beaded trim
White thread; sewing machine
Medium-weight paper in purple and white
Crafts knife; computer; glue stick
Cloud-patterned scrapbook paper

here's how

1 Cut a 5¾×6¼-inch piece from velour paper. Measure 1 inch from a short end and fold the paper. Make a ¼-inch tuck under the fold. Slip the ribbon from the beaded trim into the tuck. Machine-stitch across paper to secure trim.

2 Draw a nine-pane window on the purple paper with each of the openings 1⅛-inch square and the grid ⅛ inch thick. Use a crafts knife to cut out panes.

3 On a computer, type and print "Have a beautiful, blue-sky kind of day!" to fit pane. Trim and glue in center pane.

4 Cut a 4⅛-inch square from cloud paper. Glue to the back of the window. Glue the window in the center of the pink paper, placing under beaded trim.

5 Glue the pink paper atop a piece of white paper. Trim ¼ inch beyond the pink paper.

6 Cut a 7×7½-inch piece of purple paper. Fold over ¼ inch at one short end. Glue the white paper in the center of the purple paper. Cut a 7×7¼-inch piece of white paper for the inside. Glue one short end to the tab on purple paper.

7 Cut a 7×1¼-inch strip from cloud paper. Glue the strip near the bottom of the inside. Choose a purchased, coordinating envelope or see *pages 62–69* for patterns for making envelopes.

Have a beautiful, blue-sky kind of day!

Gold Medallion Card

A lacy gold sticker looks like jewelry atop pretty coordinating papers.

3 coordinating papers: gold card stock, lightweight gold, and vellum
Ruler; crafts knife; glue stick
Gold sticker
Gold glitter dimensional fabric paint
Kneaded eraser

here's how

1 Cut gold card stock to measure 5½×5 inches. Cut translucent paper to 5½×5¾ inches. Cut gold paper strip to 5½×1½ inches.

2 Fold a 1½-inch flap along the 5½-inch edge of the translucent paper. Apply glue to flap and attach to top of gold card.

3 Glue the gold paper strip on translucent paper along fold. Apply gold sticker. Write "happy birthday" with glitter paint. Let dry.

Envelope

1 Use a purchased envelope or use the pattern on *page 63*. Enlarge and trace the pattern; cut out. Trace around the pattern on envelope paper. Cut out with crafts knife and ruler.

2 To score the fold lines, lightly run knife along ruler placed on fold lines, barely breaking the surface of the paper.

3 Erase any pencil lines with kneaded eraser. Fold in flaps and glue in place with glue stick. Apply sticker to flap.

Envelope Patterns

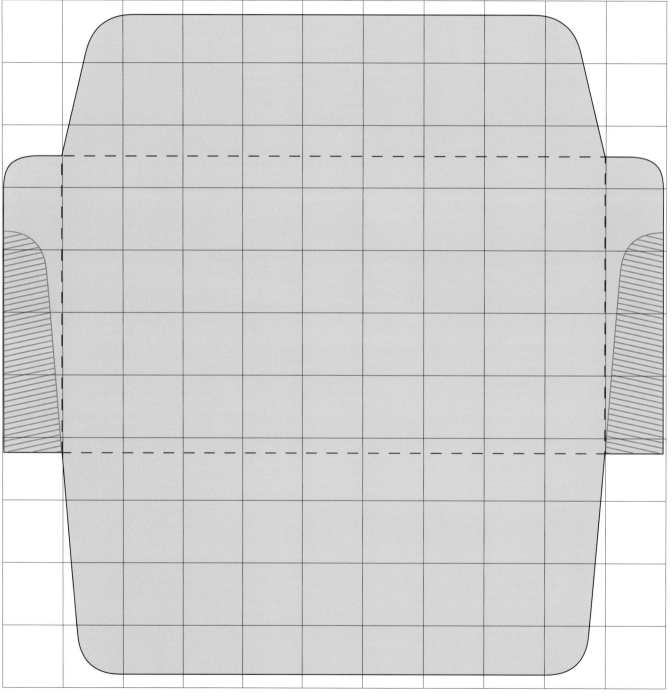

DELIGHTFUL DAISY ENVELOPE PATTERN *(pages 8–9)*

1 SQUARE = 1 INCH

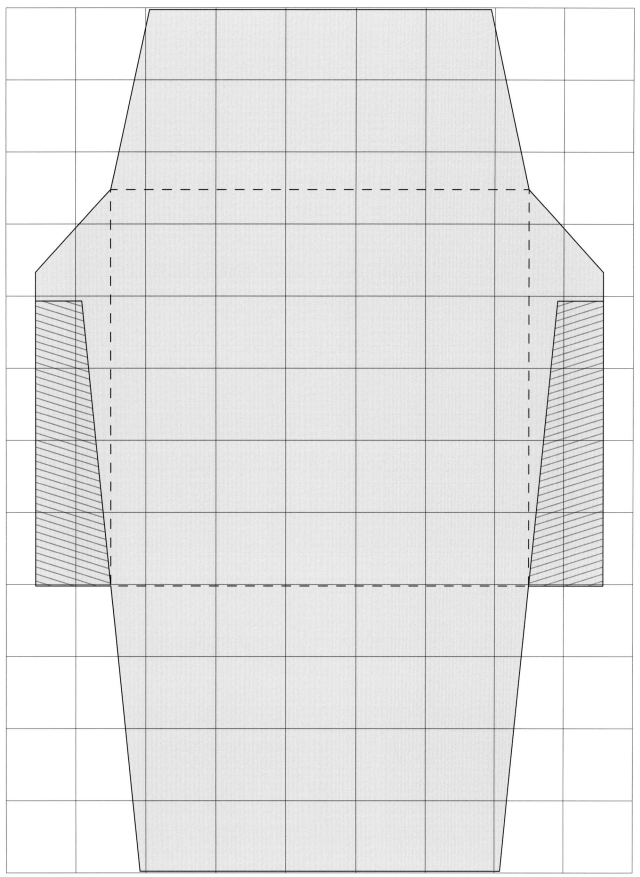

GOLD MEDALLION CARD ENVELOPE PATTERN *(pages 60–61)*   **1 SQUARE = 1 INCH**

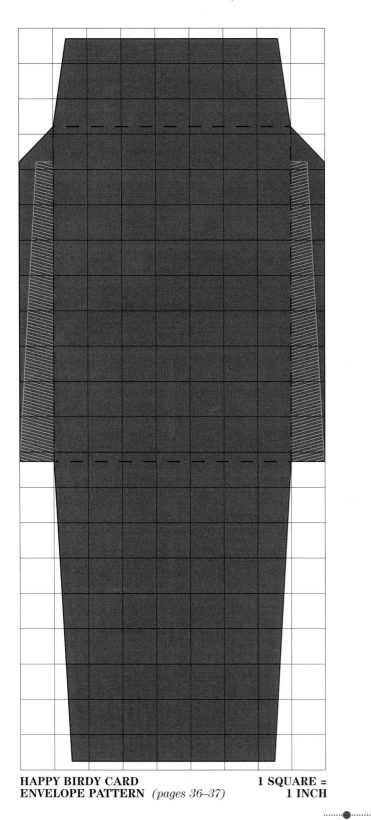

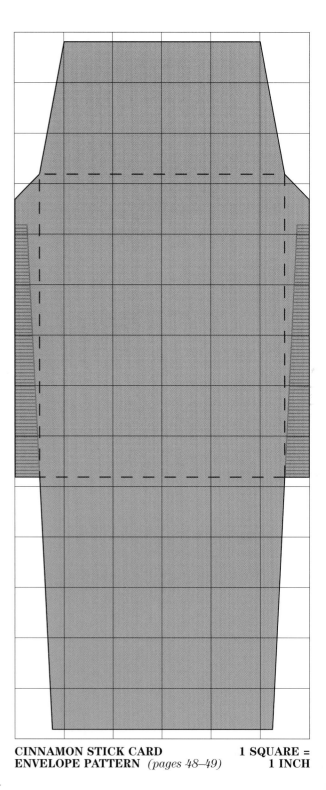

HAPPY BIRDY CARD
ENVELOPE PATTERN *(pages 36–37)*

1 SQUARE =
1 INCH

CINNAMON STICK CARD
ENVELOPE PATTERN *(pages 48–49)*

1 SQUARE =
1 INCH

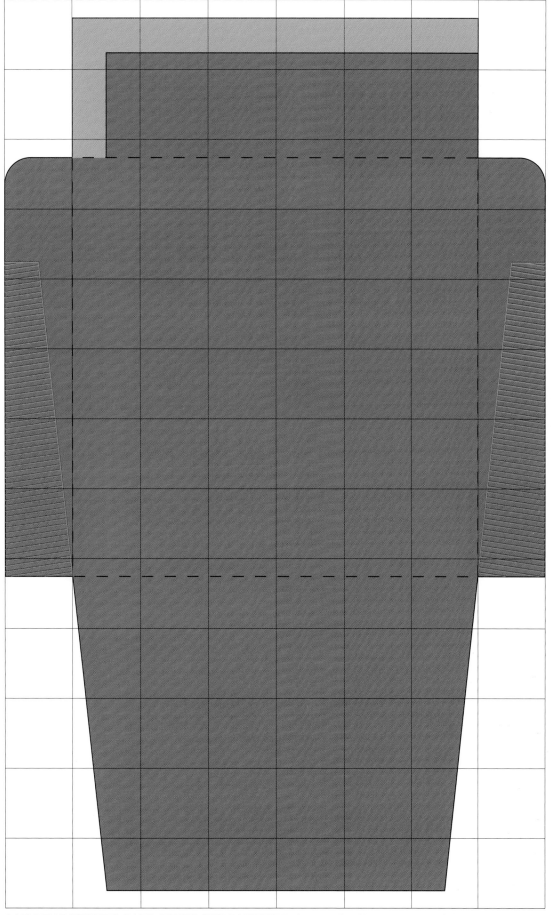

OAK LEAF WISHES CARD ENVELOPE PATTERN *(pages 18–19)*   1 SQUARE = 1 INCH

Envelope Patterns continued

DIE-CUT CARD ENVELOPE PATTERN *(page 34)*

1 SQUARE = 1 INCH

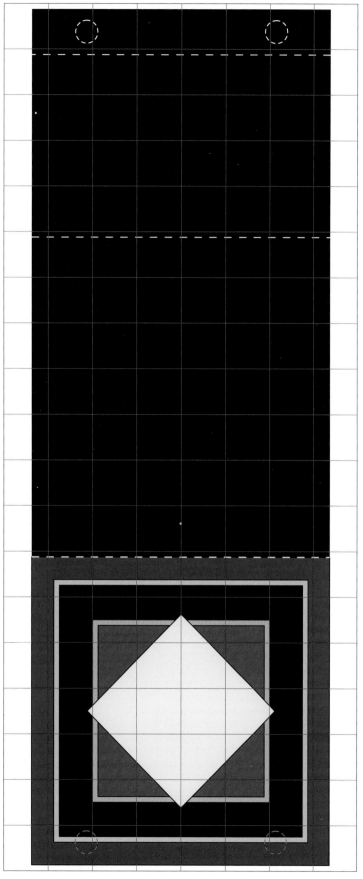

YOU'RE A STAR CARD
PATTERNS *(pages 14–15)*

1 SQUARE = 1 INCH

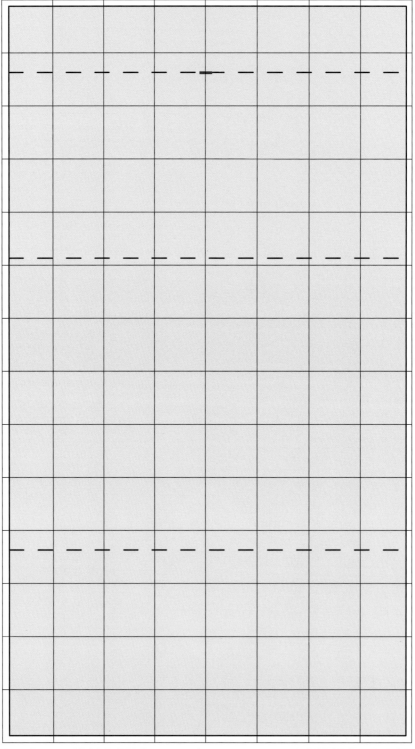

ARTFUL MESSAGE CARD
ENVELOPE PATTERN *(pages 40–41)*

1 SQUARE = 1 INCH

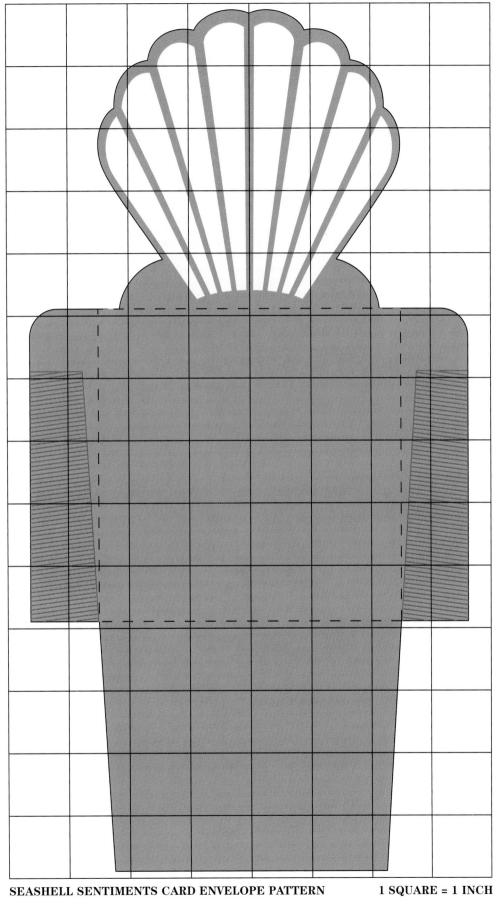

SEASHELL SENTIMENTS CARD ENVELOPE PATTERN
(pages 24–25)

1 SQUARE = 1 INCH

For more cake ideas, visit the Recipe Center at www.bhg.com/bkrecipe

Cakes

The grand finale of every birthday party is blowing out the candles—and these sweet creations taste as spectacular as they look! From playful dinosaurs to fondant-wrapped packages, you're sure to find a wonderful design that takes the cake.

Garden Mosaic Cake

Like sparkling glass in a garden stepping-stone, candies add the same beautiful luster to the top of this carrot cake.

what you'll need
- 1 recipe Carrot Cake
- 1 recipe Cream Cheese Frosting
- 1 to 2 pounds clear, hard, colored candy

carrot cake
- 2 cups all-purpose flour
- 2 cups sugar
- 1 teaspoon baking powder
- 1 teaspoon baking soda
- 1 teaspoon ground cinnamon
- 3 cups finely shredded carrots
- 1 cup cooking oil
- 4 eggs

1 Preheat oven to 350°F. Grease and lightly flour two 9×1½-inch round baking pans; set pans aside.

2 In a large mixing bowl combine flour, sugar, baking powder, baking soda, and cinnamon. Add carrots, oil, and eggs. Beat with an electric mixer until combined. Pour batter into prepared pans.

3 Bake in preheated oven for 30 to 35 minutes or until a wooden toothpick comes out clean. Cool cakes in pans on wire racks for 10 minutes. Remove cakes from pans. Cool completely on racks.

cream cheese frosting
- 2 3-ounce packages cream cheese, softened
- ½ cup butter or margarine, softened
- 2 teaspoons vanilla
- 4½ to 4¾ cups sifted powdered sugar

1 Beat together cream cheese, butter, and vanilla until light and fluffy. Gradually add 2 cups of the powdered sugar, beating well. Gradually beat in enough of the remaining powdered sugar to reach spreading consistency.

how to decorate

1 Make colored "tile" pieces by placing clear, hard candies in a heavy-duty plastic bag. This works best if each color of candy has its own plastic bag. Place a kitchen towel on top and under plastic bag. With a meat mallet or hammer, gently break the candies into coarse pieces. Remove candy dust by placing the broken candy in a wire sieve. Working over a large bowl, shake out dust and small pieces of candy; discard. On a flat surface, practice arranging some candy pieces into a garden design as once candy is placed in frosting it will be difficult to move.

2 To assemble, place one cake layer on a cake plate. Frost cake layer with some of the Cream Cheese Frosting. Add the second cake round. Frost top and sides of cake. If desired, using a decorating bag fitted with a ribbon tip, pipe an edge around bottom of cake.

3 While frosting is still wet, create your garden design with broken pieces of clear hard candies. In general, it is better to start in the center and work your way to the edge. Cover and store in refrigerator. Cake serves 12 to 16.

Pretty Package Cake

Fondant in subtle shades of green makes beautiful wrapping for this delicious cake. Stack the layers on a glass pedestal dish for a grand presentation.

what you'll need

- 2 **recipes Yellow Cake**
- 1 **recipe Creamy White Frosting**
- 3 **24-ounce boxes of prepared fondant**
  Paste food coloring in leaf green and
  royal blue
- 2 **tablespoons water**
- 2 **teaspoons meringue powder**

yellow cake

- 2½ **cups all-purpose flour**
- 2½ **teaspoons baking powder**
- ½ **teaspoon salt**
- ⅔ **cup butter or margarine**
- 1¾ **cups sugar**
- 1½ **teaspoons vanilla**
- 2 **eggs**
- 1¼ **cups milk**

1 Grease and lightly flour two 6-inch square cake pans and two 9-inch square cake pans; set pans aside.*

2 Preheat oven to 375°F. Combine flour, baking powder, and salt; set aside. In a large mixing bowl beat butter with an electric mixer on medium to high speed for 30 seconds. Add sugar and vanilla; beat until well combined. Add eggs, one at a time, beating 1 minute after each. Add flour mixture and milk alternately to butter mixture, beating on low speed after each addition just until combined. Pour batter into prepared pans.

3 Bake in preheated oven for 30 to 35 minutes or until a wooden toothpick comes out clean. Cool cakes in pans on wire racks for 10 minutes. Remove cakes from pans. Cool completely on racks.

*Note: You will need to make two separate cake recipes to make all the cake layers.

yellow cupcakes

for use on pages 90–95

1 To make cupcakes, grease and lightly flour thirty 2½-inch muffin cups or line with paper baking cups. Prepare cake as directed *left,* in Step 2. Fill each cup half full. Bake in preheated oven for 18 to 20 minutes or until a wooden toothpick inserted in center of a cupcake comes out clean. Cool on a wire rack. Serves 30.

creamy white frosting

- 1 **cup shortening**
- 1½ **teaspoons vanilla**
- ½ **teaspoon lemon extract, orange extract,**
  or almond extract
- 4½ **cups sifted powdered sugar**
- 3 **to 4 tablespoons milk**

1 Beat shortening, vanilla, and extract with an electric mixer on medium speed for 30 seconds. Gradually add half of the powdered sugar, beating

instructions continued on page 76

Pretty Package Cake continued

well. Add 2 tablespoons of the milk. Gradually beat
in remaining powdered sugar and enough remaining
milk to reach spreading consistency.

how to decorate

1 To tint fondant, add a tiny amount of paste food
coloring with a toothpick and knead fondant
with your hands until even in color. Tint two boxes
of the fondant very lightly. Tint the last box of
fondant a shade darker. Keep fondant covered with
plastic wrap when not using.

2 To assemble 6-inch cake, spread a small
amount of frosting on top of one cake layer.
Add the second cake layer. Spread a thin layer of
frosting over sides and top. Frosting does not need
to completely cover the cake. It only helps the
fondant stick to the cake. Keep frosted cake
covered to prevent it from drying out. Repeat with
9-inch cake layers.

3 To cover cakes with fondant, on a surface
lightly dusted with powdered sugar, roll out

one light-colored portion of fondant to a circle
about ¼ inch thick and 14 inches in diameter. You
may sprinkle additional powdered sugar over top of
rolled fondant to keep it from sticking to rolling
pin. Gently loosen the bottom of rolled fondant.
Transfer to top of 6-inch cake. Lightly smooth and
flatten fondant against the sides of cake, allowing
excess fondant to gather at corners of cake. With
kitchen shears, make one vertical cut to remove
excess fondant at corners and smooth cut with
fingers dusted with powdered sugar. With a smooth
knife edge or metal spatula, trim excess fondant at
bottom edge of cake. Knead the excess fondant
into your second portion of fondant. Cover the
9-inch frosted cake the same way, except roll out
fondant to a 17-inch diameter. If rolling out
fondant on a cutting board, you may find it easier
to transfer fondant by holding cutting board over
cake and sliding fondant into place. Or you may
transfer fondant by loosely rolling it onto your
rolling pin, then unrolling the fondant onto the cake.

4 To prepare the 9-inch cake to hold the
weight of the 6-inch cake, you will need to
insert about five straws into the center 6 inches of
the 9-inch cake. Before inserting the five straws,
cut them exactly the same length, which should
also be the height of the 9-inch cake.

5 To make bow and ribbon, on a surface lightly
dusted with powdered sugar, roll out the
darker tinted fondant to about ⅛-inch thickness.
Try to roll the fondant into a 12-inch square.
With a knife, smooth pastry wheel, or pizza cutter,
cut fondant into 1½-inch-wide strips. Cut all but
three strips into lengths that are 6 inches long.
(Cover the remaining three strips and set aside.)
You should get at least 13 pieces.

6. Cover several cardboard tubes (from paper towels or wrapping paper) with foil. Wrap the 6-inch lengths of fondant into loops around tubes, letting ends meet. In a very small dish, whisk together 2 tablespoons water and 2 teaspoons meringue powder until frothy and well combined. Brush mixture onto the ends of loops where they meet as shown *opposite*. Press together to seal. Let dry overnight. Cover and chill meringue powder mixture for use in a later step. When loops are dry, carefully slide them off the foil-covered tubes. Trim the ends of the loops with a sharp knife so that they come to a point.

7. To assemble cake, place the 6-inch cake on top of the 9-inch cake, resting the small cake on the straws for support. Uncover the three reserved strips of fondant. Piece two of the strips to resemble a ribbon cascading down two sides of the stacked cakes. After arranging and cutting the strips, brush the undersides lightly with some of the reserved meringue powder mixture and gently press them to the sides of cakes. Use the third strip of fondant to make end pieces of ribbon that are notched at the ends. Attach to cake as with other ribbon pieces.

8. For bow, arrange about six of the dried loops as close together as possible in a ring on top of small cake, pointed ends toward the center. Where any loops touch, brush lightly with some meringue powder mixture. Stack a second ring of four or five loops on top of the first ring. Again, lightly brush any places that touch with some meringue powder mixture. Finally, place one or two more loops in the center top of the bow. Keep cake lightly covered until ready to serve. Cake serves 20.

Birthday Song Cake

Chocolate music notes dance across the top of this marble cake,
adding a festive touch to the creamy butter frosting.

what you'll need
- 1 recipe Marble Cake
- 1 recipe Butter Frosting
- 2 ounces chocolate-flavored candy coating

marble cake
- 2 cups all-purpose flour
- 1½ teaspoons baking powder
- ½ teaspoon baking soda
- ¼ teaspoon salt
- ¾ cup butter or margarine
- 1¼ cups sugar
- 2 teaspoons vanilla
- 2 eggs
- 1 cup milk
- ⅓ cup chocolate-flavored syrup

1 Preheat oven to 350°F. Grease and flour a
13×9×2-inch baking pan; set pan aside.
Combine flour, baking powder, baking soda, and
salt; set aside.

2 In a large mixing bowl beat butter for
30 seconds. Add sugar and vanilla; beat until
fluffy. Add eggs, one at a time, beating well after
each. Add flour mixture and milk alternately to
beaten mixture, beating on low speed after each
addition just until combined.

3 Transfer 1½ cups of the batter to another
bowl; stir in chocolate-flavored syrup. Pour
light-color batter into prepared pan. Spoon
chocolate batter atop. With a thin metal spatula or
table knife, gently cut through batters to marble.

4 Bake in preheated oven for 30 to 35 minutes
or until a wooden toothpick comes out clean.
Cool cake in pan for 10 minutes on a wire rack.
Invert onto a serving platter. Cool completely.

butter frosting
- ⅓ cup butter or margarine
- 4½ cups sifted powdered sugar
- ¼ cup milk
- 1½ teaspoons vanilla
- Milk
- 1 tablespoon unsweetened cocoa powder

1 In a mixing bowl beat butter with an electric
mixer on medium speed until fluffy. Gradually
add 2 cups of the powdered sugar, beating well.
Slowly beat in the ¼ cup milk and vanilla. Beat in
remaining powdered sugar. Beat in additional milk,
if needed, to reach spreading consistency. Remove
⅓ cup of the frosting to a small bowl. Stir in
unsweetened cocoa powder and enough milk to
make frosting a creamy consistency.

how to decorate

1 To decorate cake, spread top and sides of cake
with enough white frosting to cover. Make
frosting smooth with a long metal spatula. Using a
cake comb or a crinkle vegetable cutter, make wavy
lines on top of cake. Place any remaining white
frosting in a decorating bag fitted with a large star
tip. Pipe swirls or shells along top and bottom

edges of cake. Place the chocolate frosting in another decorating bag fitted with a small round tip for writing. Pipe your birthday message onto top of cake.

2 To make chocolate standing music notes, in a small saucepan melt the chocolate-flavored candy coating over low heat, stirring often. Cool until warm, not hot, and pour into a disposable plastic decorating bag. Cover a cookie sheet with a piece of waxed paper. Snip tip of decorating bag to make a very small opening. Pipe various music notes onto waxed paper. Chill about 5 minutes, until hard. Carefully peel music notes from waxed paper. Arrange them on decorated cake. Cake serves 12 to 16.

Chocolate Decadent Cake

Surprise a chocolate lover with this candy-topped treat. Beneath the truffle frosting is moist German chocolate cake layered with caramel cream filling.

what you'll need

- 1 recipe German Chocolate Cake
- 1 recipe Caramel Cream Filling
- 1 recipe Truffle Frosting
- 6 to 8 purchased filled chocolate candies
- 1 1-ounce milk chocolate bar

german chocolate cake

- 1½ cups all-purpose flour
- ¾ teaspoon baking soda
- ¼ teaspoon salt
- 1 4-ounce package sweet baking chocolate
- ½ cup water
- 1 cup sugar
- ¾ cup shortening
- 3 eggs
- 1 teaspoon vanilla
- ¾ cup buttermilk or sour milk*

1 Preheat oven to 350°F. Grease and lightly flour two 8×1½-inch or 9×1½-inch round baking pans; set pans aside. Stir together flour, baking soda, and salt; set aside.

2 In a saucepan combine chocolate and water. Cook and stir over low heat until melted; cool.

3 In a bowl, beat sugar and shortening with a mixer on medium to high speed until fluffy. Add eggs and vanilla; beat on low until combined. Beat on medium for 1 minute. Beat in chocolate mixture. Add flour mixture and buttermilk alternately to beaten mixture, beating on low after each addition just until combined. Pour batter into prepared pans.

4 Bake in preheated oven about 30 minutes for 9-inch layers, 35 to 40 minutes for 8-inch layers, or until a wooden toothpick comes out clean. Cool cakes in pans on wire racks for 10 minutes. Remove cakes from pans. Cool completely on wire racks.

*Note: If you don't have buttermilk on hand, substitute sour milk in the same amount. For the ¾ cup of sour milk needed, place 2¼ teaspoon *lemon juice or vinegar* in a glass measuring cup. Add enough *milk* to make ¾ cup total liquid; stir. Let the mixture stand for 5 minutes before using it in a recipe.

caramel cream filling

- ⅔ cup packed brown sugar
- 1 tablespoon cornstarch
- ¼ cup apple cider or apple juice
- ¼ cup butter
- 1 egg yolk, beaten
- 1 8-ounce package cream cheese

1 In a small saucepan combine the brown sugar and cornstarch. Add apple cider and butter. Cook and stir over medium heat until thickened and bubbly. Cook and stir for 2 minutes more. Remove from heat.

2 Gradually stir ½ cup of the hot brown sugar mixture into beaten egg yolk. Add the egg mixture to the saucepan. Cook and stir until bubbly; reduce heat. Cook and stir for 2 minutes more. Remove from heat; cover and cool.

3 In a bowl beat the cream cheese until fluffy. Gradually beat in ½ cup of caramel sauce.

Cover and chill remaining sauce for up to five days. Serve over apple slices, ice cream, or poached fruit.

truffle frosting

- 1½ **cups whipping cream**
- ¼ **cup light-colored corn syrup**
- 1 **12-ounce package (2 cups) semisweet chocolate pieces**
- 1 **teaspoon vanilla**

1 In a heavy medium saucepan bring whipping cream and corn syrup to a simmer. Remove from heat. Stir in chocolate pieces and vanilla; let stand for 2 minutes. Whisk mixture until smooth and melted. Cover and chill about 1½ hours or until mixture is easy to spread, stirring occasionally. Beat with an electric mixer on medium speed until fluffy.

how to decorate

1 To assemble, place one of the cake layers bottom side up on a serving platter. Spread Caramel Cream Filling over top of cake layer on platter. Place second layer, bottom side down, on top of filling. Spread Truffle Frosting onto the sides and top of cake. Place any remaining Truffle Frosting in a decorating bag fitted with a medium star tip. Pipe shells or swirls onto top edge of cake.

2 Decorate cake top with purchased chocolate candies. To make chocolate curls, the chocolate bar should be just warmer than room temperature. Holding a vegetable peeler at an angle, pull it across the side of chocolate bar. Let curl fall into a dish; do not touch curls or they may melt. Use a toothpick to transfer curls to cake. Cake serves 12 to 16.

Baby Doll Cake

A girl at any age would be thrilled to have this lemon-glazed pound cake as the center of attention at her birthday party.

what you'll need
- 1 recipe Pound Cake
- 1 recipe Lemon Icing
  Light pink and light blue sanding sugar
- 1 recipe Creamy White Frosting (see page 74)
- 1 6- to 8-inch plastic doll (without clothes)
  Liquid or paste food coloring in pink and/or blue (optional)

pound cake
- 1 cup butter
- 1 8-ounce package cream cheese
- 6 eggs
- 3 cups all-purpose flour
- 1 teaspoon baking powder
- ¼ teaspoon salt
- 2¼ cups sugar
- 2 teaspoons vanilla

1 Allow butter, cream cheese, and eggs to stand at room temperature for 30 minutes. Meanwhile, grease and lightly flour a 10-inch fluted cake pan; set aside. Combine flour, baking powder, and salt; set aside.

2 Preheat oven to 325°F. In a large mixing bowl beat butter and cream cheese with an electric mixer on medium to high speed about 30 seconds or until softened. Gradually add sugar, 2 tablespoons at a time, beating on medium speed about 5 minutes or until very light and fluffy. Add vanilla. Add eggs, one at a time, beating on low to medium speed 1 minute after each addition and scraping bowl frequently. Gradually add flour mixture, beating on low speed just until combined. Pour batter into prepared pan.

3 Bake in the preheated oven about 75 minutes or until a wooden toothpick inserted near center comes out clean. Cool cake in pan on wire rack for 15 minutes. Remove from pan. Cool completely on wire rack.

lemon icing
- 3 cups sifted powdered sugar
- 1 teaspoon finely shredded lemon peel
- 2 to 4 tablespoons lemon juice

1 In a small bowl stir together powdered sugar, finely shredded lemon peel, and lemon juice to make icing of a pouring consistency.

how to decorate

1 Place cake on a wire rack over a jelly roll pan. Spoon icing over cooled cake to completely cover. If necessary, reuse icing that runs off cake. While icing is still wet, sprinkle cake with light pink and light blue sanding sugar.

2 Fill center of cake with frosting. Insert plastic doll into frosting in center of cake. With metal spatula or spoon, add enough frosting around base of doll to join doll to cake. Place frosting in a decorating bag fitted with medium to large rose tip. Pipe ruffles over doll's shoulders. Add other dress details using rose tip and/or a medium round tip. To make bonnet, pipe dots to cover top of doll's head. With rose tip, add a ruffle around edge of bonnet and dress bottom. Pipe a ribbon tie for bonnet using a small rose tip. If desired, tint a small amount of frosting with pink and/or blue food coloring. Use a small round tip to pipe tiny bows on skirt of doll dress. Cake serves 16.

Flower Power Car Cake

This bright cake will please any teen.
Change the wheels and add some numbers and you could transform this car
into one that's ready for racing.

what you'll need

- 1 recipe Devil's Food Cake
- ½ recipe Creamy White Frosting (see page 74)
  Liquid or paste food coloring in green or other desired color
- 4 chocolate sandwich cookies
- 1 green licorice twist
  Assorted small candies
  Purchased candy flower decorations (optional)
- 1 long slender candle (optional)

devil's food cake

- 2¼ cups all-purpose flour
- ½ cup unsweetened cocoa powder
- 1½ teaspoons baking soda
- ¼ teaspoon salt
- ½ cup shortening
- 1¾ cups sugar
- 1 teaspoon vanilla
- 3 eggs
- 1⅓ cups cold water

1 Preheat oven to 350°F. Grease and lightly flour two 9×1½-inch round baking pans; set pans aside. Stir together flour, cocoa powder, baking soda, and salt; set aside.

2 In a large mixing bowl beat shortening with an electric mixer on medium to high speed for 30 seconds. Add sugar and vanilla; beat until well combined. Add eggs, one at a time, beating well after each. Add flour mixture and water alternately to beaten mixture, beating on low speed after each addition just until combined. Pour batter into prepared pans.

3 Bake in preheated oven for 35 to 40 minutes or until a wooden toothpick comes out clean. Cool cakes in pans on wire racks for 10 minutes. Remove cakes from pans. Cool completely on wire racks. Place one cake layer in a freezer bag for later use. Seal, label, and freeze for up to three months.

devil's food cupcakes

for use on pages 96–97

1 To make cupcakes, grease and lightly flour thirty 2½-inch muffin cups or line with paper baking cups. Prepare cake as directed. Fill each cup half full. Bake in preheated oven for 15 to 20 minutes or until a wooden toothpick inserted in center of a cupcake comes out clean. Cool on a wire rack.

how to decorate

1 Arrange cooled cake layer with bottom side up. Spread the bottom side with a small amount of frosting. Cut cake layer in half and fold the two halves up to join together. You will have a half circle of two layers of cake that is sitting on its side. With a long serrated knife, cut a small L-shape notch from the cake between about one and two o'clock

on the cake. This forms the windshield and hood of the car. Transfer to a serving plate.

2 Tint the remaining frosting light green or other desired color with food coloring. Remove about ½ cup of the frosting and tint it a darker shade of green or desired color. Place the darker frosting in a decorating bag fitted with a small round tip. Frost entire cake with light green

frosting. Pipe details onto car with the darker green frosting in the decorating bag. Attach cookie wheels with some frosting. Attach licorice and other candies with a small amount of frosting to make bumpers, wheel covers, and headlights on car. If desired, insert the slender candle to serve as an antenna. Cake serves 6.

Fishbowl Cake

Shaped like a fishbowl, this clever cake is sure to bring cheers. The candies at the bottom add color and texture beneath the frosted fish.

what you'll need

- 1 recipe White Confetti Cake
- 1 recipe Creamy White Frosting (see page 74)
  Liquid or paste food coloring in peach and blue
- 1 cup small pebblelike candies, such as Nerds
- 1 purchased tube blue piping gel

white confetti cake

- 2 cups all-purpose flour
- 1 teaspoon baking powder
- ½ teaspoon baking soda
- ⅛ teaspoon salt
- ½ cup shortening, butter, or margarine
- 1¾ cups sugar
- 1 teaspoon vanilla
- 4 egg whites
- 1⅓ cups buttermilk or sour milk*
- ¼ cup multicolored nonpareils

1 Preheat oven to 350°F. Grease and lightly flour two 8×1½-inch round baking pans; set pans aside. Stir together flour, baking powder, baking soda, and salt; set aside.

2 In a large mixing bowl beat shortening with an electric mixer on medium to high speed for 30 seconds. Add sugar and vanilla; beat until well combined. Add egg whites, one at a time, beating well after each. Add flour mixture and buttermilk alternately to beaten mixture, beating on low speed after each addition just until combined. Stir in nonpareils. Pour batter into prepared pans.

3 Bake in preheated oven for 30 to 35 minutes or until a wooden toothpick comes out clean. Cool cakes in pans on wire racks for 10 minutes. Remove cakes from pans; cool completely on racks.

*Note: If you don't have buttermilk on hand, substitute sour milk in the same amount. For the 1⅓ cup of sour milk needed, place 1 tablespoon *lemon juice or vinegar* in a glass measuring cup. Add enough *milk* to make 1⅓ cup total liquid; stir. Let the mixture stand for 5 minutes before using it in a recipe.

how to decorate

1 Set aside about ⅓ cup frosting for making fish. Tint remaining frosting a light blue using liquid or paste food coloring. Tint the ⅓ cup frosting peach using food coloring.

2 Spread about ½ cup blue frosting on the bottom side of one of the cake rounds. Top with second cake round, placing it bottom side down. With a sharp serrated knife, remove a 1-inch slice from one side of cake. This will make a flat place for the bottom of fishbowl. Then make another thin slice on opposite side of cake for top of fish bowl. Carefully stand up cake and place on serving plate. With a small metal spatula spread blue frosting over cake. While frosting is still moist, press small pebblelike candies into frosting at bottom of cake.

3 Place the peach frosting in a decorating bag fitted with a medium rose tip. Pipe an oval

shape for fish body. Make little ruffles for fish tails and fins. Place remaining blue frosting in a decorating bag fitted with a large star tip. Pipe a border at top of fishbowl. If desired, add a small round tip and pipe stripes on fish. Using blue piping gel, pipe bubbles above the fish. Cake serves 12.

Quilted Cake

Here's an artful idea that's as pretty as a stitched quilt. Once the pattern is established, paint on the miniature patterns with a brush.

what you'll need
- 1 recipe Hot-Milk Sponge Cake
- 1 recipe Lemon Butter Frosting
- 12 ounces prepared fondant
  - Vodka
  - Paste food coloring

hot-milk sponge cake
- 1 cup all-purpose flour
- 1 teaspoon baking powder
- 2 eggs
- 1 cup sugar
- ½ cup milk
- 2 tablespoons butter or margarine

1 Preheat oven to 350°F. Grease and flour a 9×9×2-inch baking pan; set pan aside. Stir together flour and baking powder; set aside.

2 In a medium mixing bowl beat eggs with an electric mixer on high speed about 4 minutes or until thick. Gradually add sugar, beating on medium speed for 4 to 5 minutes or until light and fluffy. Add the flour mixture; beat on low to medium speed just until combined.

3 In a small saucepan heat and stir milk and butter until butter melts. Add milk mixture to batter, beating until combined. Pour batter into prepared pan.

4 Bake in preheated oven for 20 to 25 minutes or until a wooden toothpick comes out clean. Cool cake in pan on a wire rack for 10 minutes. Remove cake from pan; cool completely on rack.

lemon butter frosting
- ⅓ cup butter or margarine
- 4½ cups sifted powdered sugar
- ¼ cup fresh lemon juice
- ½ teaspoon finely shredded lemon peel
- 1½ teaspoons vanilla
  - Milk
  - Liquid or paste food coloring (optional)

1 In a mixing bowl beat butter until fluffy. Gradually add 2 cups of the powdered sugar, beating well. Slowly beat in the lemon juice, lemon peel, and vanilla.

2 Slowly beat in remaining powdered sugar. Beat in milk, if needed, to reach spreading consistency. If desired, tint with food coloring.

how to decorate

1. Reserve about 1 cup of frosting for piping. On a cake plate, frost top and sides of cake using the remaining frosting. The frosting on top of cake can be a thin layer.

2. To make "quilt" layer, on a surface dusted with powdered sugar, roll out fondant to a 9-inch square, about ¼ inch thick. Trim fondant, if necessary, to get a perfect square shape. Using a smooth pastry wheel and ruler, score the top of cake into a quilt design as shown on *page 88*. Be sure pastry wheel only marks fondant without cutting all the way through.

3. To make "paint", for each color place about 1 tablespoon vodka in a very small dish. (Note: Vodka is used because its high alcohol content causes it to evaporate quickly on the fondant without dissolving fondant or allowing colors to bleed. Water would make the fondant very wet and sticky, and colors would bleed.) Add paste food coloring (this cake is yellow, navy, and light blue) to dishes and stir to dissolve. Paint your designs on quilted fondant using clean art brushes or cotton swabs.

4. With a long metal spatula, gently loosen fondant from surface. Transfer to top of cake. Place ½ cup of the reserved frosting in a decorating bag fitted with a large star tip. Pipe a border on top edge of cake. If desired, tint remaining ½ cup frosting a coordinating color and use same tip to pipe a border on bottom edge of cake. Cake serves 9.

Bug's World Cupcakes

Made from flattened gumdrops, these sugary bugs
make colorful toppers for individual cakes. Use the ideas here
or create your own edible bugs.

what you'll need

1 recipe Yellow Cupcakes (see page 74) or
   1 recipe Devil's Food Cupcakes (see page 84)
1 recipe Creamy White Frosting (see page 74)
   Small colored gumdrops
   Sugar
   Brown liquid or paste food coloring

BUMBLEBEE

DRAGONFLY

LADYBUG

how to decorate

1 Frost cupcakes with frosting. If desired, place some of frosting in a decorating bag fitted with a star, rose, or round tip. Pipe desired border on cupcakes. Top with gumdrop bugs below. Decorated cupcakes can be frozen up to two weeks before serving.

2 To make any of the gumdrop decorations, on a surface sprinkled with sugar, roll out gumdrops to about ⅛-inch thickness. Keep gumdrop from sticking to rolling pin by sprinkling additional sugar on top of gumdrop while rolling. After shaping, press decorations into frosting.

3 *For ladybug,* roll out a red gumdrop and cut into a circle using greased kitchen shears* or 1½-inch round cookie cutter. Cut the red circle almost in half to make wings. Use a half circle of purple for head. Pipe dots of brown frosting on wings. *For dragonfly,* roll out orange and green gumdrops. Cut out an orange body and green wings. *For bumblebee,* roll out a yellow gumdrop and a purple gumdrop until not quite ⅛ inch thick. Cut both gumdrops into skinny strips. Lay strips side by side, alternating yellow and purple colors. Press

them together to stick. Resugar surface and top and reroll to ⅛-inch thickness. Cut an oval body from striped gumdrop. Roll out another yellow gumdrop and cut wings and antennae.

*Note: To grease kitchen shears, cutters, or knife to keep from sticking, just spray lightly with nonstick coating.

Flower Cupcakes

As dainty as fresh-picked blossoms, these candy flowers add pretty
pastel touches against white frosting.

what you'll need

1 recipe Yellow Cupcakes (see page 74) or
1 recipe Devil's Food Cupcakes (see page 84)

1 recipe Creamy White Frosting (see page 74)
Small colored gumdrops; sugar

how to decorate

1. Frost cupcakes with frosting. If desired, place some of the frosting in a decorating bag fitted with a star, rose, or round tip. Pipe desired frosting border on cupcakes. Top with gumdrop flowers (directions *below*). Decorated cupcakes can be frozen up to two weeks before serving.

2. For each gumdrop decoration you will need 2 to 4 small gumdrops. To make any of the gumdrop decorations, on a surface sprinkled with sugar, roll out gumdrops to about ⅛-inch thickness. Keep gumdrops from sticking to rolling pin by sprinkling additional sugar on top of gumdrops while rolling. After shaping the decorations, press them into frosting on cupcakes.

3. *For rosebud,* roll out pink gumdrops and cut oval petals (about 1×¾ inch). Roll up first petal jelly-roll-style. Wrap second petal around first. Slightly curl top edge of petal out. Add a third petal around outside and curl the top edge out. Pinch off excess gumdrop at bottom of rose. Roll out green gumdrops and cut out leaf shapes using kitchen shears* or small leaf cutters. *For tulip,* roll out orange, yellow, pink, or purple gumdrops. Cut out teardrop shapes (about 1×¾ inch) using kitchen shears. Lay first petal on work surface with point up. Add two more petals on top with their points slightly turned out. Add two more petals on top with their points even more turned out. Press all the petals together to stick. Roll out a green gumdrop and cut out slender leaves; arrange at bottom of tulip. *For pansy,* roll out purple gumdrops and yellow gumdrops. (For a bicolor effect you can roll out a colored gumdrop and a white gumdrop together, slightly overlapping.) Cut out 1-inch round petals. With fingers, pinch a pleat on one side of each petal. Place two yellow and two purple petals together. Arrange all four with pleats to center. Pinch them all together. Add green leaves.

*Note: To grease kitchen shears, cutters, or knife to keep from sticking, just spray lightly with nonstick coating.

ROSE BUD

TULIP

PANSY

Fruity Cupcakes

Sugared gumdrop fruits make each of these cupcakes a delight to make and to eat!

what you'll need

1   recipe **Yellow Cupcakes** (see page 74) or
    1 recipe **Devil's Food Cupcakes** (see page 84)
1   recipe **Creamy White Frosting** (see page 74)
    Small colored gumdrops; sugar

how to decorate

1 Frost cupcakes with frosting. If desired, place some of the frosting in a decorating bag fitted with a star, rose, or round tip. Pipe desired frosting border on cupcakes. Top with gumdrop fruit (directions *below*). Decorated cupcakes can be frozen up to two weeks before serving.

2 For each gumdrop decoration, you will need 2 to 4 small gumdrops. To make any of the gumdrop decorations, on a surface sprinkled with sugar, roll out gumdrops to about ⅛-inch thickness. Keep gumdrops from sticking to rolling pin by sprinkling additional sugar on top of gumdrops while rolling. After shaping the decorations, press them into frosting on cupcakes.

3 *For cherries,* roll out red gumdrops and cut into ¾-inch circles. Roll out green gumdrops and cut out shapes for stems and a leaf. Frosting on cupcake will hold cherries in place. *For pineapple,* roll out a yellow gumdrop to about ¼-inch thickness. With a greased sharp knife*, score in a diamond pattern. Sprinkle with some additional sugar. Roll out a green gumdrop and cut out pineapple top with kitchen shears. *For pear,* make a two-toned piece of rolled gumdrop. Roll out two colors (yellow and green, orange and yellow, etc.) of gumdrops at the same time, slightly overlapping them as you begin to roll. Continue to sprinkle with sugar to keep from sticking. Cut

CHERRIES

PINEAPPLE

PEAR

out a 2-inch pear shape with kitchen shears.
Add a green leaf and yellow stem using more
rolled gumdrops.

*Note: To grease kitchen shears, cutters, or knife
to keep from sticking, just spray lightly with
non-stick coating.

P.B. Bear

For those who love the taste of peanut butter, this adorable character bares the perfect solution.

what you'll need

1 recipe Peanut Butter Cake and 1 recipe Peanut Butter Cupcakes or 1 recipe Devil's Food Cake and 1 recipe Devil's Food Cupcakes (see page 84)
2 recipes Butter Frosting (see page 78)
 Paste food coloring in brown and yellow
 Yellow and pink jimmies or oblong sprinkles
 Yellow gumdrops

peanut butter cake

2 cups all-purpose flour
1 cup packed brown sugar
2 teaspoons baking powder
½ teaspoon baking soda
¼ teaspoon salt
1 cup milk
½ cup peanut butter
2 eggs
¼ cup butter or margarine, softened

1 Preheat oven to 375°F. Grease and lightly flour two 9×1½-inch round baking pans; set pans aside.

2 In a large mixing bowl stir together the flour, brown sugar, baking powder, baking soda, and salt. Add milk, peanut butter, eggs, and butter. Beat with an electric mixer on low speed until combined. Beat on medium to high speed for 3 minutes, scraping bowl frequently. Spoon batter into the prepared pans, spreading evenly.

3 Bake in preheated oven about 30 minutes or until a wooden toothpick comes out clean. Cool cakes in pans for 30 minutes. Remove cakes from pans. Cool completely on wire racks.

peanut butter cupcakes

1 Grease and lightly flour thirty 2½-inch muffin cups or line with paper baking cups. Prepare cake as directed, *left*. Fill each cup half full. Bake in preheated oven for 18 to 20 minutes or until a wooden toothpick inserted in center of cupcake comes out clean. Cool on a wire rack.

how to decorate

1 You will need six or seven of the cupcakes for bear cake. Remaining cupcakes can be frosted as desired and served with cake. Tint about ⅓ cup of the frosting brown using paste food coloring. Leave about one-third of the frosting plain. Tint remaining frosting yellow using paste food coloring.

2 Arrange the two round cake layers on a serving platter, one round for the head and one round for the body. Trim six cupcakes to make a flat side on each so that they fit snugly against round cakes. Place two on

head for ears and four on body for paws. If desired, a seventh cupcake may be used for bear's nose. Cut the top off a cupcake. Turn it upside down and place on bear's face.

3 Frost entire bear with yellow frosting. While frosting is still moist, sprinkle with yellow and pink jimmies. For pads on bear's paws, cut yellow gumdrops in half and press the cut side into frosting on paws. Place the white and the brown frosting in decorator bags fitted with small to medium round decorating tips. Use white to pipe oval eyes on bear face. Use brown to pipe dots on eyes and to make mouth and nose. There will be extra frosting left over to decorate cupcakes. Cake serves 18, plus there will be 23 additional cupcakes.

Apple Dino Cake

Kids love dinosaurs, and this polka-dotted apple-spice fellow will make birthday boys or girls giggle with delight!

what you'll need

1   recipe Applesauce Spice Cake or
    1 recipe Devil's Food Cake (see page 84)
1   recipe Creamy White Frosting
    (see page 74)
    Paste or liquid food coloring in green
    Small green gumdrops, halved
    Candy-coated milk chocolate pieces

applesauce spice cake

2   cups all-purpose flour
1½   teaspoons baking powder
½   teaspoon baking soda
1   teaspoon ground cinnamon
¼   teaspoon ground nutmeg
¼   teaspoon ground cloves
¼   teaspoon ground ginger
¼   cup butter or margarine, softened
¼   cup shortening
1½   cups sugar
½   teaspoon vanilla
2   eggs
¼   cup buttermilk or sour milk*
1   cup applesauce

1 Preheat oven to 350°F. Grease and lightly flour two 8×1½-inch round baking pans; set pans aside. Stir together flour, baking powder, baking soda, cinnamon, nutmeg, cloves, and ginger; set aside.

2 In a large mixing bowl beat butter and shortening with an electric mixer on medium to high speed for 30 seconds. Add sugar and vanilla; beat until well combined. Add eggs, one at a time, beating well after each. Add flour mixture, buttermilk and applesauce alternately to beaten mixture, beating on low speed after each addition just until combined. Pour into prepared pans.

3 Bake in preheated oven for 30 to 35 minutes or until a wooden toothpick comes out clean. Cool cakes on wire racks for 10 minutes. Remove cakes from pans. Cool completely on wire racks.

Note: If you don't have buttermilk on hand, substitute sour milk in the same amount. For the ¼ cup of sour milk needed, place ¾ teaspoon *lemon juice or vinegar* in a glass measuring cup. Add enough *milk* to make ¼ cup total liquid; stir. Let the mixture stand for 5 minutes before using it in a recipe.

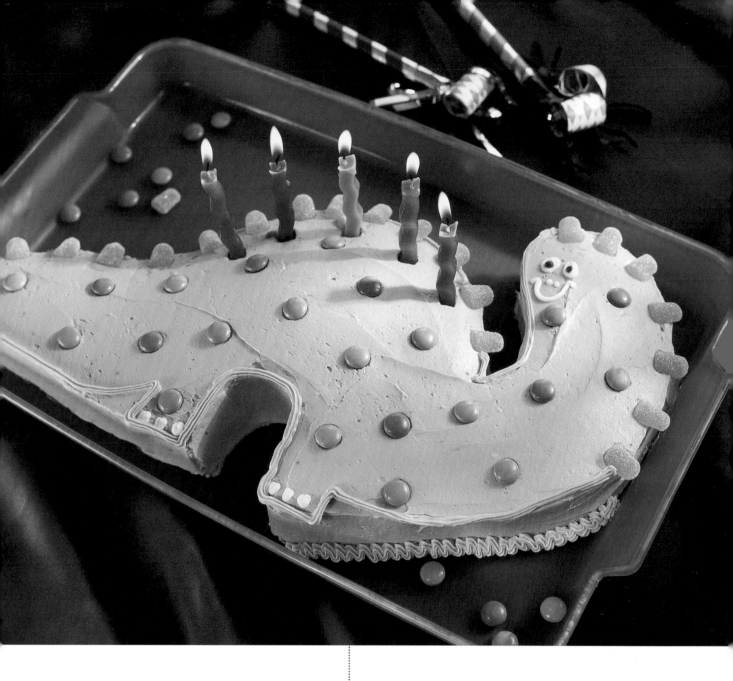

how to decorate

1. With a serrated knife, cut one of the cake rounds in half, making two half circles. Sculpt one half circle into the neck of dinosaur (see photo, *opposite*) and the other half circle into the tail of dinosaur (see photo, *opposite*). For the body of dinosaur, remove a small U-shape piece from the edge of other cake round (see photo, *opposite*). On a serving plate arrange these three pieces to make a dinosaur shape.

2. Set aside about ¼ cup frosting for eyes and feet. Tint remaining frosting with green food coloring. Frost entire cake with green frosting.

Place the ¼ cup white frosting in a decorating bag fitted with a small round tip. Pipe eyes on face and dots on feet of dinosaur. Make spikes on back of dinosaur with halved pieces of green gumdrops. Press candy-coated milk chocolate pieces into frosting to make dots on dinosaur. Cake serves 12.

Puppy Pumpkin Cake

Spice cake is always a hit with kids, so this adorable puppy is destined to be a real crowd pleaser. Chocolate candies and a licorice-stick tail add darling details.

what you'll need

1   **recipe Pumpkin Spice Cake or**
    1 recipe Devil's Food Cake (see page 84)
1   **recipe Creamy White Frosting**
    (see page 74)
    Paste food coloring in brown
    Round chocolate-covered mints
    Candy-coated milk chocolate pieces
    Licorice stick

pumpkin spice cake

2	**cups all-purpose flour**
1½	**teaspoons baking powder**
½	**teaspoon baking soda**
1	**teaspoon ground cinnamon**
¼	**teaspoon ground nutmeg**
¼	**teaspoon ground cloves**
¼	**teaspoon ground ginger**
¼	**cup butter or margarine, softened**
¼	**cup shortening**
1½	**cups sugar**
½	**teaspoon vanilla**
2	**eggs**
1	**cup buttermilk or sour milk***
½	**cup canned pumpkin**

1 Preheat oven to 350°F. Grease and lightly flour two 8×1½-inch round baking pans; set aside. Stir together flour, baking powder, baking soda, cinnamon, nutmeg, cloves, and ginger; set aside.

2 In a large mixing bowl beat butter and shortening with an electric mixer on medium to high speed for 30 seconds. Add sugar and vanilla; beat until well combined. Add eggs, one at a time, beating well after each. Add flour mixture, buttermilk, and canned pumpkin alternately to beaten mixture, beating on low speed after each addition just until combined. Pour into prepared pans.

3 Bake in preheated oven for 30 to 35 minutes or until a wooden toothpick comes out clean. Cool cakes in pans on wire racks for 10 minutes. Remove cakes from pans. Cool completely on wire racks.

*Note: If you don't have buttermilk on hand, substitute sour milk in the same amount. For each cup of sour milk needed, place 1 tablespoon *lemon juice or vinegar* in a glass measuring cup. Add enough *milk* to make 1 cup total liquid; stir. Let the mixture stand for 5 minutes before using it in a recipe.

how to decorate

1 With a serrated knife, trim a small scallop from one cake and a U shape from the second cake. Place cakes together on a serving tray as shown in photo, *opposite*. Cut each cake cutout in half and arrange halves on cake to make ears and feet (see photo, *opposite*).

2 Set aside ¼ cup of the frosting. Tint the ¼ cup frosting with brown food coloring. Frost entire cake with the remaining white frosting. Place the

brown frosting in a decorating bag fitted with a medium round tip. Pipe dog's face, feet, and any other details onto cake. Add spots using chocolate-covered mints, eyes and a tongue using candy-coated milk chocolate pieces, and a tail using a licorice stick. Cake serves 12.

Snowflake Cake

A gorgeous treat for any winter birthday, this pretty cake is blanketed in fondant embellished with cookie-cutter snowflakes.

what you'll need

- 1 recipe White Chocolate Cake
- 1 recipe Creamy White Frosting (see page 74)
- 1½ 24-ounce boxes prepared fondant (36 ounces total)

  Paste food coloring in blue

  Assorted snowflake cookie cutters

  Clear edible glitter and/or sanding sugar

  Powdered sugar

white chocolate cake

- 4 egg whites
- 1¾ cups all-purpose flour
- 2 teaspoons baking powder
- ¼ teaspoon salt
- 3 ounces white chocolate baking bar, chopped
- ¾ cup half-and-half, light cream, or milk
- ⅓ cup butter or margarine
- 1 cup sugar
- 1½ teaspoons vanilla
- 4 egg yolks

1 In a mixing bowl allow egg whites to stand at room temperature for 30 minutes. Meanwhile, grease and lightly flour two 8×1½-inch round baking pans; set pans aside. Stir together flour, baking powder, and salt; set aside.

2 In a heavy small saucepan melt the chopped white chocolate baking bar with ¼ cup of the half-and-half over very low heat, stirring constantly until baking bar starts to melt. Immediately remove from heat; stir until baking bar is completely melted and smooth. Stir in remaining half-and-half; cool.

3 Preheat oven to 350°F. In a large mixing bowl beat the butter with an electric mixer on medium to high speed for 30 seconds. Add sugar and vanilla; beat until well combined. Add egg yolks, one at a time, beating until combined. Add the flour mixture and white chocolate baking bar mixture alternately to beaten mixture, beating on low to medium speed after each addition just until combined.

4 Wash the beaters. Beat egg whites with an electric mixer on high speed until stiff peaks form (tips stand straight). Gently fold egg whites into the batter. Spread batter in the prepared pans.

5 Bake in preheated oven for 25 to 30 minutes or until a wooden toothpick comes out clean. Cool cakes in pans on wire racks for 10 minutes. Remove cakes from pans. Cool completely on racks.

how to decorate

1 To assemble, place one cake layer on a cake plate. Frost cake layer with some of the frosting. Add the second cake layer and frost top and sides

of cake. Add a very small amount of blue paste food coloring to two-thirds of the fondant (24 ounce). Knead with your hands until color is uniform. Keep all fondant wrapped with plastic wrap until needed.

2 To cover cake with fondant, on a surface lightly dusted with powdered sugar, roll out the light blue fondant to about ¼-inch thickness and a circle about 14 inches in diameter. You may sprinkle additional powdered sugar over top of rolled fondant to keep it from sticking to rolling pin. Gently loosen the underside of rolled fondant. Loosely roll fondant onto rolling pin. Transfer to top of cake. Lightly smooth and flatten fondant against the sides of cake, allowing excess fondant to gather at bottom of cake. With a smooth knife edge or metal spatula, trim excess fondant at bottom edge of cake.

3 On surface dusted with powdered sugar, roll out the remaining half box of white fondant (12 ounces) to ⅛ inch thickness. Trim to an 11-inch circle. Make delicate snowflake cutouts in fondant using assorted snowflake cookie cutters. With a long metal spatula, gently loosen fondant from surface. With pastry brush, lightly brush top of cake with water. Transfer snowflake fondant to top of cake (see photo, *opposite*). Lightly press to seal to cake top. If desired, use the cutout scraps to decorate bottom edge of cake. Use pastry brush to lightly brush backs of snowflake cutouts with water, then stick them onto cake. To add extra sparkle to cake top, sprinkle cake with clear edible glitter and/or sanding sugar. Cake serves 12.

Edible Flower Delight

For a quick-to-decorate cake blooming with personality, top the cake
with a mini bouquet of fresh herbs and pansies.

what you'll need

1 **recipe Banana Cake**
1 **recipe Cream Cheese Frosting**
   (see page 73)
   Lavender paste food coloring
   Fresh herbs and/or edible flowers, such as
   lavender, flowering thyme, sage, mint,
   pansies, mini roses, and violets
   Narrow ribbon

banana cake

2¼ **cups all-purpose flour**
1½ **cups sugar**
1½ **teaspoons baking powder**
1 **teaspoon baking soda**
½ **teaspoon salt**
1 **cup mashed ripe bananas (about 3)**
¾ **cup buttermilk or sour milk***
½ **cup shortening**
1 **teaspoon vanilla**
2 **eggs**

1 Preheat oven to 350°F. Grease and lightly flour
two 8×1½-inch or 9×1½-inch round baking
pans; set pans aside.

2 In a large mixing bowl stir together flour, sugar,
baking powder, baking soda, and salt. Add
bananas, buttermilk, shortening, and vanilla. Beat
with an electric mixer on low speed until
combined. Add eggs; beat on medium speed for
2 minutes. Pour batter into prepared pans.

3 Bake in preheated oven for 25 to 30 minutes
or until a wooden toothpick comes out clean.
Cool cakes in pans on wire racks for 10 minutes.
Remove cakes from pans. Cool completely on racks.

*Note: If you don't have buttermilk on hand,
substitute sour milk in the same amount. For the
¾ cup of sour milk needed, place 2¼ teaspoons
lemon juice or vinegar in a glass measuring cup.
Add enough *milk* to make ¾ cup total liquid; stir.
Let the mixture stand for 5 minutes before using it
in a recipe.

how to decorate

1 Set ½ cup frosting aside. To assemble, place
one cake layer on a cake plate. Frost cake layer
with some of the frosting. Add the second cake
layer and frost top and sides of cake.

2 Place the ½ cup reserved frosting in a
decorating bag fitted with a medium to large
rose tip. With a zigzag motion, make a wavy border
on top edge of cake. Tint any remaining frosting
with lavender paste food coloring. With lavender
frosting placed in decorating bag fitted with small
round tip, pipe birthday message at edge of cake
top. Cover and store cake in refrigerator.

3 Just before serving, tie together a small
bouquet of pesticide-free fresh herbs and
pansies, or other flowers, with a narrow ribbon.
Cake serves 12 to 16.

Playing Cards Cake

Bid fun birthday greetings to your favorite card player
with this delicious cake.

what you'll need

- 1 **recipe Citrus Yellow Cake**
- 1 **recipe Whipped Cream Frosting**
- 1 **recipe Raspberry Filling**
  Chocolate-flavored candy coating discs
  Red candy coating discs
- 8 **ounces vanilla-flavored candy coating**

citrus yellow cake

- 2½ **cups all-purpose flour**
- 2½ **teaspoons baking powder**
- ½ **teaspoon salt**
- ⅔ **cup butter or margarine**
- 1¾ **cups sugar**
- 1½ **teaspoons vanilla**
- 2 **eggs**
- 1¼ **cups milk**
- 2 **teaspoons finely shredded orange peel or**
    lemon peel

1 Preheat oven to 375°F. Grease and lightly flour
two 8×1½-inch or 9×1½-inch round baking
pans; set pans aside. Combine flour, baking powder,
and salt; set aside.

2 In a large mixing bowl beat butter with an
electric mixer on medium to high speed for
30 seconds. Add sugar and vanilla; beat until well
combined. Add eggs, one at a time, beating
1 minute after each. Add flour mixture and milk
alternately to beaten mixture, beating on low speed
after each addition just until combined. Stir orange
peel into batter. Pour batter into prepared pans.

3 Bake in preheated oven for 30 to 35 minutes
or until a wooden toothpick comes out clean.
Cool cakes in pans on wire racks for 10 minutes.
Remove cakes from pans. Cool completely on racks.

whipped cream frosting

- 2 **cups whipping cream**
- ⅔ **cup dairy sour cream**
- ¼ **cup sifted powdered sugar**
- 1 **teaspoon vanilla**

1 For frosting, in a chilled large mixing bowl, beat
the whipping cream, sour cream, powdered
sugar, and vanilla until stiff peaks form.

raspberry filling

- 1 **10-ounce package frozen raspberries in**
    syrup, thawed
- 4 **teaspoons cornstarch**

1 In a small saucepan combine raspberries in
syrup with cornstarch. Cook and stir until
thickened and bubbly; reduce heat. Cook and
stir for 2 minutes more. Remove from heat.
Immediately press through wire sieve; discard
seeds. Transfer to bowl. Cover surface of filling with
plastic wrap. Chill, without stirring, at least 2 hours
or overnight.

how to decorate

1. Arrange cooled cake layers with bottom sides up. Spread each with a small amount of the frosting. Spread Raspberry Filling on top of one of the cake layers. Invert the remaining cake layer and place on top of the filling-covered cake layer.

2. Transfer cake to a serving plate. Frost sides and top generously with the remaining frosting. If desired, place some frosting in a decorating bag fitted with a large star tip. Pipe frosting along the top edge of cake. Cover loosely and chill until serving time, up to 24 hours.

3. Meanwhile, prepare garnish. Line a cookie sheet with waxed paper; set aside. In very small microwave-safe bowls, melt the chocolate and red candy coating discs. Transfer to disposable decorating bags. Snip a very small hole in end of each bag. Pipe chocolate spades and clubs onto the waxed paper. Pipe red hearts and diamonds onto same piece of waxed paper. Chill about 10 minutes or until designs are hard. Melt vanilla-flavored candy coating in the microwave or in a small saucepan over low heat. Working quickly, pour evenly over half of the chilled designs and spread gently to an even thickness. Leave half of your piped designs uncovered. Shake the cookie sheet gently to smooth out the melted candy coating layer. Chill until set.

4. To unmold designs, gently peel waxed paper from the back of the candy coating. Set aside the designs that are separate and open. You will also have a sheet of vanilla candy coating that has designs piped on the back side. Turn it over onto a cutting board. Use a warm sharp knife to cut the sheet into small rectangles that each have a design. Decorate each piece of cake with a few open designs and a few rectangles (cards). Cake serves 12.

Artist's Cake

Resting on a picture frame, this painterly cake is splattered with birthday wishes.
Wavy candles add a creative touch to the special dessert.

what you'll need

- 1 **recipe Chocolate Cake**
- 1 **recipe Butter Frosting (see page 78)**
- 1 **24-ounce box prepared fondant**
  Paste food coloring in three colors
  Vodka
- 2 **clean small paintbrushes**
  11×14-inch frame and a 11×14-inch
  masonite board covered with foil (optional)

chocolate cake

- ¾ **cup butter, softened**
- 3 **eggs**
- 2 **cups all-purpose flour**
- ¾ **cup unsweetened cocoa powder**
- 1 **teaspoon baking soda**
- ¾ **teaspoon baking powder**
- ½ **teaspoon salt**
- 2 **cups sugar**
- 2 **teaspoons vanilla**
- 1½ **cups milk**

1 Allow butter and eggs to stand at room
temperature for 30 minutes. Meanwhile, grease
and flour one 13×9×2-inch baking pan. In a
medium bowl stir together flour, cocoa powder,
baking soda, baking powder, and salt; set aside.

2 Preheat oven to 350°F. In a large mixing bowl
beat butter with an electric mixer on medium
to high speed for 30 seconds. Gradually add sugar,
about ¼ cup at a time, beating on medium speed
until well combined (3 to 4 minutes). Scrape sides
of bowl; continue beating on medium speed for
2 minutes. Add eggs, one at a time, beating after
each addition (about 1 minute total). Beat in vanilla.

3 Alternately add flour mixture and milk to
butter mixture, beating on low speed after
each addition just until combined. Beat on medium
to high speed for 20 seconds more. Spread batter
evenly into the prepared pan.

4 Bake in preheated oven for 35 to 40 minutes or
until a wooden toothpick inserted near the
center of the cake comes out clean. Cool cake in
pan for 10 minutes; remove from pan. Invert onto
picture frame and board or serving platter.

how to decorate

1 Frost the top and sides of the cake. Set the
cake aside.

2 Working on a surface dusted with powdered
sugar, lightly knead prepared fondant. Using
toothpicks, add streaks of paste food coloring to
surface of fondant. Use at least three colors of food
coloring, making several streaks of each. Again,
lightly knead fondant just until the colors begin to
marble. Dust surface again with powdered sugar.
With a rolling pin, roll out the fondant to a
rectangle about 15×12 inches. Loosely roll fondant
around rolling pin and transfer to top of frosted
cake. Lightly smooth and flatten fondant against
the sides of cake, allowing excess fondant to gather
at corners of cake. With kitchen shears, make one
vertical cut to remove excess fondant at corners.
Smooth cut with fingers dusted with powdered

sugar. With a knife edge or metal spatula, trim excess fondant at bottom edge of cake.

3 For splatter-paint technique, for each color, in a very small bowl stir together about 1 tablespoon vodka and about ⅛ teaspoon paste food coloring. Cover any areas on or around cake where you don't want paint to splatter. Dip tip of a pastry brush into paint. Holding paint bowl above cake, drag dipped pastry brush across edge of bowl, allowing paint to splatter onto cake. If desired, repeat with other paint colors. Write a message on top of cake using a clean small art brush and more paint. Lay a couple of brushes on top for decorations. If desired, use a picture frame as a serving platter and place on torn canvas splattered with food coloring. Cake serves 12.

Just-Fore-You Golf Cake

For those who treasure their days on the course,
this playful cake is a real winner.

what you'll need

1 **recipe White Cake**
1 **recipe Creamy White Frosting (see page 74)**
 Paste food coloring in green and brown
 Sugar ice cream cone
 Long slender candle

white cake

2 **cups all-purpose flour**
1 **teaspoon baking powder**
½ **teaspoon baking soda**
⅛ **teaspoon salt**
½ **cup shortening, butter, or margarine**
1¾ **cups sugar**
1 **teaspoon vanilla**
4 **egg whites**
1⅓ **cups buttermilk or sour milk***

1 Preheat oven to 350°F. Grease and lightly flour two 8×1½-inch round baking pans and two 6-ounce custard cups; set pans aside. Stir together flour, baking powder, baking soda, and salt; set aside.

2 In a large mixing bowl beat shortening with an electric mixer on medium to high speed for 30 seconds. Add sugar and vanilla; beat until well combined. Add egg whites, one at a time, beating well after each. Add flour mixture and buttermilk alternately to beaten mixture, beating on low speed after each addition just until combined. Pour batter evenly into prepared pans and cups.

3 Bake in preheated oven for 30 to 35 minutes or until a wooden toothpick comes out clean.

Cool on wire rack for 10 minutes. Remove cakes from pans and cups. Cool completely on wire racks.

***Note:** If you don't have buttermilk on hand, substitute sour milk in the same amount. For the 1⅓ cups of sour milk needed, place 1 tablespoon plus 1 teaspoon *lemon juice or vinegar* in a glass measuring cup. Add enough *milk* to make 1⅓ cups total liquid; stir. Let the mixture stand for 5 minutes before using it in a recipe.

how to decorate

1 Tint two-thirds of the frosting green using paste food coloring. Tint about ¼ cup of the white frosting brown using paste food coloring. Use about ½ cup white frosting to spread on the bottom side of one of the cake rounds. Top with second cake round placing it bottom side down. Place on cake plate. Use the green frosting to frost cake sides and top.

2 To make golf tee, gently insert a sugar ice cream cone into the cake top. Use a serrated knife to trim any corner edges left by the custard cups on small cakes. To make golf ball, spread a small amount of white frosting onto the top of one custard cup cake. Turn other custard cup cake over and place on top so that the two tops are together. Place remaining white frosting in a decorating bag fitted with a small star tip. Pipe some frosting onto top edge of cone. Place golf ball cake on top, pressing into frosting. Pipe white stars over golf ball cake to cover.

3 Place remaining green frosting in a decorating bag fitted with a large leaf tip to create large, long blades of grass at bottom of tee and at edge of cake. Use leaf tip to make a wavy border at bottom edge of cake. Use a writing tip and brown frosting to add writing on the cake. If desired, decorate a long, slender candle with a paper flag. Cake serves 12.

Sweet 16 Cake

It's fun to do something special for significant birthdays. For young ladies turning 16, this cake will never be forgotten.

what you'll need

- 1 recipe Coconut White Cake
- 1½ recipes Creamy White Frosting*
  (see page 74—*Note: Use ½ teaspoon coconut extract instead of vanilla.)
- ¼ cup pineapple preserves or other preserves
  Paste or liquid food coloring in pink
- 1 purchased tube pink writing gel

coconut white cake

- 2 cups all-purpose flour
- 1 teaspoon baking powder
- ½ teaspoon baking soda
- ⅛ teaspoon salt
- ½ cup shortening, butter, or margarine
- 1¾ cups sugar
- 1 teaspoon vanilla
- 4 egg whites
- ¼ cup flaked coconut
- 1⅓ cups buttermilk or sour milk**

1 Preheat oven to 350°F. Grease and lightly flour two 8×1½-inch round baking pans; set the pans aside. Stir together flour, baking powder, baking soda, and salt; set aside.

2 In a large mixing bowl beat shortening with an electric mixer on medium to high speed for 30 seconds. Add sugar and vanilla; beat until well combined. Add egg whites, one at a time, beating well after each. Stir flaked coconut into batter. Add flour mixture and buttermilk alternately to beaten mixture, beating on low speed after each addition just until combined. Pour batter into the prepared pans.

3 Bake in preheated oven for 30 to 35 minutes or until a wooden toothpick comes out clean. Cool cakes in pans on wire racks for 10 minutes. Remove layer cakes from pans; cool completely on racks.

Note: If you don't have buttermilk on hand, substitute sour milk in the same amount. For the 1⅓ cups of sour milk needed, place 1 tablespoon plus 1 teaspoon *lemon juice or vinegar* in a glass measuring cup. Add enough *milk* to make 1⅓ cups total liquid; stir. Let the mixture stand for 5 minutes before using it in a recipe.

how to decorate

1 If desired, cut each cake layer in half, horizontally. Spread the ¼ cup pineapple or other preserves between each set of halved layers. Tint frosting light pink using food coloring.

2 To assemble, place one cake layer on a cake plate. Frost cake layer with some of the pink frosting. Add the second cake layer. Frost top and sides of cake, using about 1 recipe frosting.

3 Place some of the remaining frosting in a decorating bag fitted with a basket-weave tip (zigzag tip). Pipe straight, vertical lines on side of cake. Change tip to a large star tip. Pipe a shell border on top edge of cake. Change tip to a small round tip. Write message on top of cake. If desired, pipe a curly vine design and add small

rosebuds using a small rose tip. Finally, add dots
on side of cake with purchased pink writing gel.
Cake serves 12.

For even more birthday ideas, go to www.bhg.com/bkhomemadebirthday

Gifts

What a joy it
is to present
someone special with the
perfect birthday gift.
And the event is even
more wonderful when the
gift is a handmade
treasure or treat made
with friendship and love.
Gifts like these
make birthdays
simply unforgettable.

Seashell Soap

Cherished gift anytime of the year, decorative soaps bring beauty to the powder room. These seaside soaps are as pretty as an ocean shore.

what you'll need

Blue glycerin soap block; knife
Glass measuring cup; white coconut oil soap block
Purchased plastic soap molds
Small seashells

here's how

1 Break the blue soap block into small pieces and place into the measuring cup.

2 Carefully slice small bird-shape and sand pieces from the white soap block. Arrange with seashells in the plastic soap molds as shown, *right*. Melt the blue soap in the microwave following the manufacturer's instructions. Let cool until a thin film appears on the top of the soap.

3 Skim film aside and pour into molds. Allow to set. Cool completely. Remove soap from molds.

MOLD PREPARATION

Butterfly Mugs

Everyone who enjoys a good cup of java will love a set of these fanciful butterfly mugs. Tuck a coffee packet or two in each cup for a welcome surprise.

what you'll need
Solid-color glass coffee mugs
Tracing paper; pencil
Transfer paper
Glass paints in black and other desired colors
Fine-tip and other paintbrushes
Pencil with round eraser

here's how
1 Wash and dry each mug. Avoid touching the areas to be painted.

2 Trace the desired patterns, *right*. Use transfer paper to transfer the patterns randomly to the mug. To make each butterfly, start with the color portion of the wings. Each wing can be a simple oval or two smaller connected ovals. Use one or two paint colors for each wing. Let dry before adding black details.

3 Using a fine-tip paintbrush, paint simple outlines for each butterfly. For each body, paint a small circle for the head with antennae and an elongated oval for the body. Add dots on the wings if desired. Let dry.

4 To add polka dots, dip the eraser of a pencil into paint and carefully dot onto the surface of the mug, placing randomly between butterflies and down the edge of the mug handle. Let dry.

BUTTERFLY PATTERNS

Dad Album

Give Dad a cleverly decorated album for storing treasured photographs, newspaper clippings, small works of art, and other cherished keepsakes.

what you'll need

Glue stick; two 9⅞×5½-inch pieces of decorative paper for outside cover
Two 6½×4½-inch pieces of mat board for covers
Two 2½×4½-inch pieces of mat board for flaps

Two 8⁵⁄₁₆×4⅜-inch pieces of decorative paper for inside cover; ⅛-inch hole punch
1-inch-wide rubber band; large paper clips
Paper scraps; buttons; press-on lettering
1 package of plastic mini pocket album refills
15-inch piece of plastic-coated telephone wire

here's how

1 Apply glue to back side of one of the cover papers. Center and lay a cover board and a flap board on paper, leaving a ⅛-inch gap between cover and flap. Fold edges of paper over edges of mat board. Repeat for other cover board and flap.

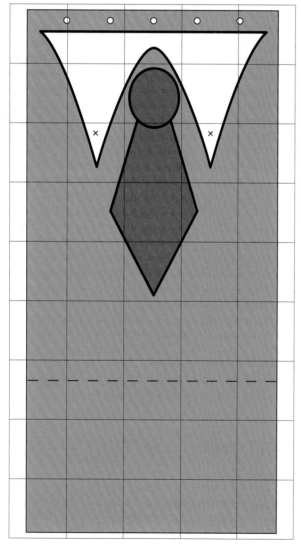

DAD ALBUM PATTERNS   1 SQUARE = 1 INCH

2) Center and glue an inside cover paper over the mat board cover/flap. When glue is entirely dry, mark five holes along top edge of cover, ¼ inch down from edge and ¾ inch apart. Use hole punch to punch holes. Do the same for the other cover/flap.

3) Decorate the front cover with press-on letters or use paper scraps and buttons to add a collar and a tie (enlarge and trace patterns, *opposite*) for a shirt.

4) Cut binder hole edge off each of the plastic mini pocket album refills. Punch holes across top edge to correspond with holes on mat board covers.

5) Sandwich the album refills between the front and back covers. Use clips to hold all together. Cut wire into 3-inch pieces. Slip a piece through each set of holes and make a circle about the diameter of a pencil. Twist the ends around each other four or five times. The twisted ends should be on the back side. Cut off excess wire.

6) Fold flaps to outside of each cover and use a rubber band to keep album closed.

7) To stand, remove rubber band from top cover flap only and flip top cover over to back. Overlap the two flaps, slipping the front flap through the rubber band on the back flap.

Embroidered Envelope

Perfect for holding a gift certificate or money, this floral envelope is a gift in itself. Later it can be used to organize coupons, magazine clippings, or photos.

what you'll need

Tracing paper
Pencil; scissors; ruler
Felt in bright pink, white, turquoise, green, purple, and orange
Black embroidery floss
Straight pins; paper punch
Scrap paper

here's how

1 Enlarge and trace the envelope and flower patterns, *below.* Cut out the pattern pieces.

2 Trace around the pattern pieces on the appropriate pieces of felt. Cut out the shapes. Cut a 7½×7¼-inch piece from the pink.

3 Use free-form cross-stitches to adjoin the straight edge of the envelope flap to one short edge of the pink rectangle.

4 Using the diagram, *below,* as a guide, pin the large round flower and the leaves in place. Use blanket stitches around each piece to secure in place. Remove pins. Add running stitches to the center of each leaf.

5 To make tiny round flowers, fold scrap paper over the desired color of felt and use a paper punch to make each circle. Sew into place using French knots. Add lazy-daisy leaves.

6 Fold up the pink felt to form a 3¼-inch pocket. Pin in place. Work blanket stitches around the edges, securing both layers together for the pocket.

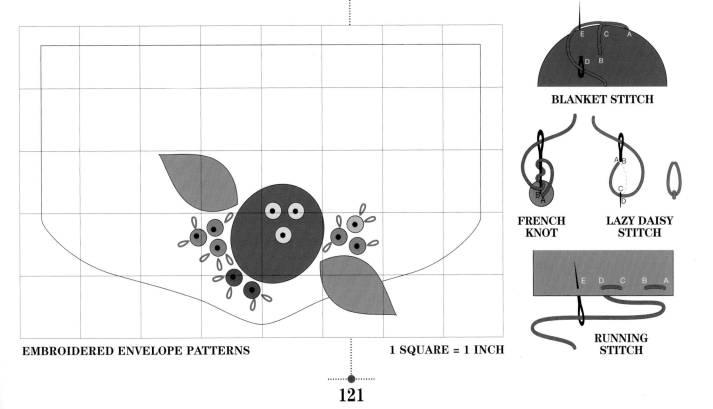

EMBROIDERED ENVELOPE PATTERNS   **1 SQUARE = 1 INCH**

BLANKET STITCH

FRENCH KNOT

LAZY DAISY STITCH

RUNNING STITCH

Party Hats

Complete with a noisemaker, these party hats are sure to start any birthday celebration rolling. Fill them with treats for a yummy surprise.

what you'll need

Tracing paper; pencil; scissors; glue stick

Card stock in assorted bright, solid colors

Scrapbook paper in assorted prints

Decorative-edge scissors

Paper punches in star, heart, or dot shapes

Stapler and staples; 1 mm white elastic cord

Assorted stickers

Spacers, such as Pop Dots

Purchased noisemakers in
  bright colors

here's how

1 Enlarge and trace the party hat pattern, *opposite,* and cut out. Using glue stick, adhere one sheet of scrapbook paper to one sheet of card stock. On wrong side, trace the party hat pattern. Cut out sides using straight scissors and the bottom using decorative-edge scissors.

2 Add a row or two of paper punches to the bottom of the hat. Carefully roll into a hat shape, overlapping the bottom edges approximately ½ inch. Secure with a single staple approximately 1 inch from the bottom. The hat will be open at the top. Cut a 12-inch length of elastic cord and staple one end on each side of hat.

3 Use stickers and paper punches to decorate the hat. Adhere the stickers to leftover scraps from the two papers used for the hat. Cut out around the stickers with desired scissors. Layer designs for dimension. Adhere to the front of hat with spacers.

4 For the noisemaker embellishments, trace the full-size pattern, *opposite,* and cut out. Trace around pattern on card stock. Cut out using straight scissors. Cut out two small circles for insertion of noisemaker. Use coordinating paper scraps from the hat to decorate the cutout, adding paper punches and stickers for embellishment. Adhere to the cutout with spacers. Carefully insert the noisemaker into the hole cutouts, trimming the openings as necessary so the noisemaker slides through easily.

PARTY HAT PATTERN 1 SQUARE = 1 INCH

NOISEMAKER TRIM PATTERN

Timely Frame

Create a clock to match any decor by using a picture frame as the clock base.
Embellish the face with cloth, ribbon, and buttons for a one-of-a-kind timepiece.

what you'll need

4-inch square piece of cardboard
Ice pick; pencil
Battery-operated clock movement for
  ⅛-inch-thick clock face; fabric glue
4-inch square piece of fabric; scissors
8 inches of decorative ribbon
Metal frame with 4-inch square opening
Hot-glue gun and hot-glue sticks
4 decorative buttons

here's how

1 Punch a hole in the center of the cardboard square by beginning the hole with an ice pick. Push a pencil through the hole to enlarge it. The shaft of the clock movement should fit easily into this hole.

2 Using fabric glue, adhere the fabric square over the cardboard. Cut a tiny hole in the center of the fabric with scissors.

3 Use fabric glue to adhere pieces of ribbon horizontally and vertically, crossing in the center of the fabric. Cut a center hole in ribbons.

4 Remove backing and glass from metal frame and replace them with the fabric-covered cardboard square.

5 Follow directions on package to install clock movement through the hole in the center of the cardboard.

6 Hot-glue buttons to the four corners of the frame.

Friendship Candle

Tell your friends how dear they are with this sweet
little reminder. Use paint markers for a quick design, and accent the
decorated votive cup with rhinestones.

what you'll need

Paper; scissors
Clear glass flowerpots in 2 sizes
Pencil; tape
Opaque paint markers for glass
Graph paper with ¼-inch squares
Rhinestones
White glue
Jelly beans

here's how

1 Cut a piece of scrap paper to fit inside of large
flowerpot. Arrange and write message on paper
and tape paper to inside of flowerpot with message
facing outward. This candle says, "Roses are red.
Violets are blue. No one is as sweet as a friend like
you!" You can also create your own saying or choose
from the list, *right*.

2 Using pattern as a guide, write message on
outside of pot with the markers.

3 For rim, cut a strip of graph paper to fit
around inside of rim and tape in place. Using
one color, create a checkered pattern by coloring in
four squares together to form a larger square and
then skipping the next four squares. Continue in
this alternating pattern to form pattern. Let the
paint dry. Outline with a contrasting color.

4 Glue a rhinestone to the intersection of two
corners. Repeat all the way around rim. Let
the glue dry.

5 Fill flowerpot with jelly beans. Place candle in
smaller flowerpot and nestle in jelly beans.

message options

Your friendship brightens each day.
You mean the world to me.
Believe in yourself. I do.
Thank you for sharing yourself with me.
I love you dear friend!

Baby Bundles

When a new bundle of joy arrives, celebrate the birth with an adorable towel roll that keeps small objects conveniently organized.

what you'll need

Hand towel, approximately 17×29½ inches
Matching thread and needle
1 yard of ½- to 1-inch-wide embroidered trim
Pins; bunny, duck, and/or flower baby buttons
Mini rickrack trim; chenille rickrack
1 yard of 1-inch-wide ribbon or 2-inch-long strip
  of touch fastener, such as Velcro

here's how

1 Working on the right side of the towel, use a sewing machine or needle and thread to stitch the embroidered trim down the length of one long edge.

2 Lay the towel right side down, placing the embroidered trim edge at bottom. Fold the length of the bottom edge up to reveal the trim and create a 7-inch-deep pocket. Pin and then stitch the folded towel together every 3 to 6 inches to create divided pockets. Before stitching the edges of the first pocket on the right-hand side of the towel together, arrange baby buttons and rickrack along the edge on the other (right) side of towel as shown, *opposite*. This edge will become the top of the rolled-up case. Stitch the desired arrangement of buttons and/or rickrack in place.

3 If you prefer to use ribbon to tie the case, fold it in half and insert the folded edge halfway down the edge of the towel. Trap the folded ribbon in the stitches when the side edges are joined together to make the last pocket. If you choose touch fasteners to attach the case together, first stitch a scrap of trim to the back of hook portion of the touch fastener. Insert one edge of this tab halfway down the edge of the towel. Trap the end of the tab in stitches when the side edges are joined together to make the last pocket. To gauge the placement of the loop portion of the Velcro, insert various items into the finished pockets. When the case is rolled up, position the loop portion to fall under the hook tab and then stitch it in place.

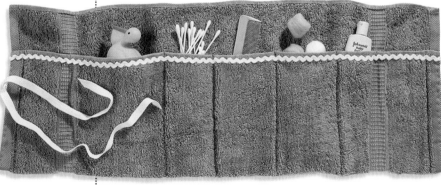

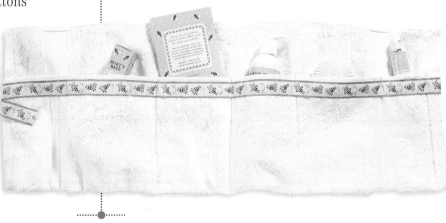

Pearlized Candle

Flea market pearls find their way into home decor with this clever candle.
This small gift is so becoming that it will beckon big thanks.

what you'll need

Small terra-cotta flowerpot
Ivory acrylic paint
Paintbrush
Pearl strands and pearl beads
Jewelry clasp
Hot-glue gun and hot-glue sticks
Ivory taper candle

here's how

1 Paint the outside and inside of the flowerpot ivory. Let the paint dry. Add a second coat if needed.

2 Wrap the outside of the flowerpot with pearl strands, using hot glue to secure in place. Glue a jewelry clasp on one side.

3 Fill the inside of the flowerpot with pearl strands or beads. Nestle the taper candle in the center of the pearls. Straighten the candle.

Sparkling Shades Case

For those fun-in-the-sun friends, a sunglass case is the just-right birthday gift.
Choose a case in a favorite hue and, in a jiffy, make it spectacular.

what you'll need

Eyeglass case with solid-color vinyl surface
Copper wide-tip permanent marker
Fine-tip markers in silver and black
Rhinestones; gem glue

here's how

1 Using a copper marker, write "shades" across the top of the eyeglass case.

2 On the left side of each letter stroke, add a thin black shadow using marker. Add a silver highlight to the right side of each letter.

3 Using the black marker, add small dots within the copper center of each letter.

4 Glue rhinestones randomly around the lettering. Let the glue dry.

Sundae Serving Set

For loved ones with a sweet tooth, paint a set of sundae dishes as a birthday treat.
These are so easy to paint; even a beginner will get rave reviews!

what you'll need

Glass sundae dishes
Glass paints in red, yellow, green, and black
Paintbrush
Pencil with round eraser

here's how

1 Wash and dry the dishes. Avoid touching the areas to be painted.

2 Turn the sundae dishes upside down. Paint the bottoms red. Let dry.

3 For each dish, paint two nickel-size red circles for the cherries. Add black stems and a simple green leaf. Paint a yellow stripe between the top and base of the sundae dish.

4 To add yellow polka dots, dip the eraser of a pencil into paint and dot on the dish base. Let the paint dry.

5 If directed by the paint manufacturer, bake the glass pieces in the oven. Let cool.

Clever Candles

When you're short on time but not on sentiment, these quick candle ideas come to the rescue. In minutes you can create either of these fun birthday gifts.

Star-Studded Candle

what you'll need
Round red candle
Eyelets in red, white, blue, and silver or gold
Star studs in silver or gold

here's how
1 Gently push studs and eyelets into candle surface. If it is difficult to push in the trims with fingers, use the back of a spoon. Continue adding trims randomly until the surface of the candle is covered.

Cellophane-Wrapped Candles

what you'll need
Scissors; ruler
Clear cellophane
3 coordinating votive candles
Sheer ribbon
Decorative shank buttons or clip earrings

here's how
1 Cut a 10-inch square from cellophane. Wrap cellophane around candles, keeping the ends even.
2 Tie the ends of the cellophane closed using ribbon. If using buttons, thread the ribbon through the shank before tying. Or clip an earring to the center of each ribbon bow.

☆Outstanding Spoons

Silverware isn't just for mealtime anymore! Make these gifts using flea market finds.

Spoon-Handle Box

what you'll need
5×2×2-inch wood box (available at crafts stores)
Acrylic paint; paintbrush
Clear acrylic sealer spray
Epoxy glue
4 marbles; buttons
Child's spoon
Hot-glue gun and hot-glue sticks

here's how
1 Base-coat the wood box with a color of your choice. Let it dry.

2 Spray the box with acrylic sealer. Let it dry.

3 Turn the base of the box upside down and glue the marbles onto the four corners of the box with epoxy glue (these will act as legs for the box). Let it dry.

4 Determine the placement of the spoon on the box lid. If desired, use epoxy to glue buttons on the lid to support the spoon handle. Hot-glue the child's spoon on the middle of the box lid. Let it dry.

Teaspoon Vase

what you'll need
4 teaspoons; hammer; 2 thick towels
Clear 1½-inch-diameter bud vase
Epoxy glue; masking tape

here's how
1 Hammer the rounded spoons flat. Place the spoons between two thick towels to eliminate damage to the work surface.

2 Bend the spoons at the base of the handles at 90-degree angles.

3 Epoxy the handles of the spoons to the bud vase so the flattened spoon heads lie flat on the table. Tape them to the vase until the epoxy glue is dry. Remove tape.

Photo Mirror

A hand mirror makes a clever frame for any endearing photograph. Trimmed with buttons and leaves, this keepsake is ready to hang.

what you'll need

Hand mirror with hole in handle; photo
Print scrapbook paper
Pencil; scissors; glue stick
Heart-shape buttons and
  plastic leaves
Thick white crafts glue
Tube-style fabric paints
  in desired colors

here's how

1 Trace around mirror area (excluding handle) on paper. Cut out slightly smaller to fit in mirror frame. Glue over mirror using a glue stick.

2 Choose a photo to place on the mirror. If necessary, enlarge or photocopy it at a copy center. Trim the photo to fit on the paper. Use a glue stick to adhere the photo in place.

3 With the handle of the mirror up and using crafts glue, arrange and glue buttons and leaves across the handle and top edge of the mirror. Let dry.

4 Add multi-color dots of paint around edge of photo and over holes in buttons. Let dry.

Designer Photo Box

As pretty as a wrapped gift and as functional as a photo album, this lidded box unfolds to reveal a collection of precious snapshots.

what you'll need

Utility knife; 4-inch-cube box with separate lid
Paper to cover box; ruler; thick white crafts glue
Large button; piece of yarn; large needle
Black adhesive photo corners
Glitter tube-style paint
Large sheet of art paper in a color to
   complement box color

here's how

1 Use a utility knife to cut down through all four corners of box so box will lie flat.

2 To cover each of the four sides, cut four pieces of paper each 1 inch larger in width and length than side of box. Center and glue paper to front of each side, folding excess paper to inside. Cut a piece of paper to fit the bottom of box and glue to box.

3 To cover lid, measure top of box and add height of sides and an additional ½ inch all around. Cut paper to this size. Center and glue paper to lid, folding paper over sides and around to inside edge. Cut a slit at each corner to ease the folding of the paper.

4 With a large needle, punch two holes in center of lid top ⅝ inch apart. Thread yarn through hole, slip button onto yarn, and tie.

5 Use adhesive photo corners and glitter paint to decorate sides of lid and corners of lid top. Let dry.

6 Cut four 3⅞×15½-inch strips from art paper. Accordion-fold strips into 3⅞-inch squares. Trim excess paper at ends.

7 Glue one end of each strip to an inside panel of box. Let glue dry. Add photo corners and photos on both sides of paper strips. Secure a photo in the bottom of the box, if desired, using photo corners.

Blooming Place Mat

Whether you make one for a dresser or a set for the kitchen, this colorful mat delivers a rainbow of joy-filled wishes.

what you'll need

Decorative-edge scissors
Crafting foam in light green, medium green, yellow, turquoise, pink, light orange, purple, and orange
Ruler; thick white crafts glue
Scissors
Tracing paper; pencil; scrap paper
Large round paper punch

here's how

1 Using decorative-edge scissors, trim the light green crafting foam to 11½×15 inches. Glue the green piece on top of a larger piece of yellow foam. Let dry.

2 Trim the sides of the yellow foam with a decorative-edge scissors and the top and bottom, if necessary, with straight-edge scissors.

3 Enlarge and trace desired patterns, *right*. Cut out patterns. Trace around patterns on desired colors of crafting foam. Glue several flowers to the upper left corner. Add flower centers and leaves as desired. Glue one or two flowers in the opposite corner.

4 To make small dots, fold a piece of scrap paper in half and sandwich the edge of a piece of crafting foam between the paper layers. Using a paper punch, punch out dots. Glue in place. Let the glue dry.

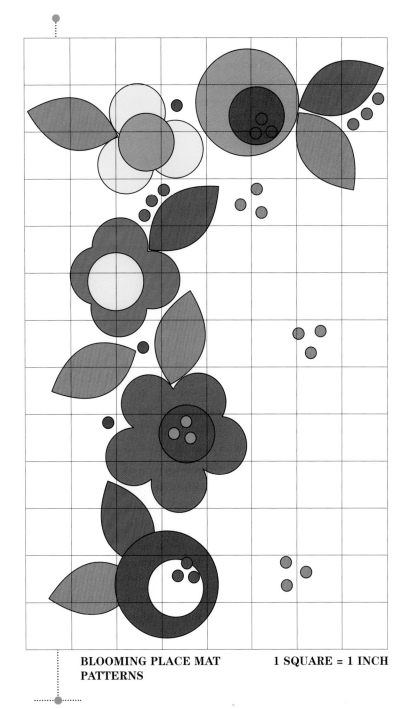

BLOOMING PLACE MAT PATTERNS   **1 SQUARE = 1 INCH**

Sentimental Stones

Send heartfelt birthday wishes by painting blissful messages on polished rocks.
Arrange them in a fountain for a grand presentation.

what you'll need
Small polished rocks
Permanent paint markers in various colors,
  such as Zig Painty markers
Plain paper; purchased fountain

here's how
1 Be sure rocks are clean. Choose words that are
  comforting or fit the message you want to
convey. Practice writing the words on plain paper.

2 Write the words on the rocks. Let dry.
  Place in fountain.

word suggestions

content	peace	love
restful	tranquil	joy
quiet	beauty	live
warmth	life	laugh

Forever Yours Journal

With a beautiful blend of color and texture, this album cover
will long be cherished.

what you'll need
Sheer white textured paper
Journal
Acrylic paint
Paintbrushes
Decoupage medium
White embroidery floss
Scissors
Assorted small beads
White glitter paint
Assorted gems and buttons
Wire cutters

here's how

1 If the paper chosen is sheer or has an open weave, use the journal as it is or paint it if desired. If painting, apply two coats of paint, allowing to dry between coats. Let dry.

2 Open the journal and lay it cover side down on the paper. Draw a line around book ½ inch larger than edge; allow for binding.

3 Apply decoupage medium to the outside of the journal. Lay the paper right side down. Paint decoupage medium on the paper. Trim the edges if needed. Fold the paper neatly around the journal and coat with decoupage medium. Let dry.

4 Cut strands of floss to drape on front. String several beads on floss in a random fashion.

5 Use white glitter paint to paint heavy dabs onto the area where buttons are desired. Press floss, gems, and buttons into paint. Let dry. If using shank buttons, snip off backs using wire cutters.

Party Pinwheels

The young at heart will love these swirly, whirly pinwheels made from seed packets. Poke them in a blooming plant for an extra special birthday present.

what you'll need
Colored pencil with eraser; ruler; seed packet
Dime; scissors; pencil
Straight pin with large plastic head
Colored beads; eraser from end of pencil

here's how

1 With a pencil and ruler, mark a line on the bottom of the seed packet to make it square. Cut off the bottom to form a square.

2 Draw pencil lines from corner to corner on the back of the paper to make an X as shown *below*. Place the dime in the center of the + on the back of the seed packet and draw around it.

3 Using scissors, cut on the lines being careful to cut only up to the drawn center circle.

4 Without folding, bend every other point to the center of the square.

5 Place a bead on the pin and push the pin through all four points of the pinwheel, one at a time, then through the center of the square.

6 Place a bead onto the pin and push the pin through the pinwheel and into the colored pencil eraser. Push an eraser onto the end of the pin as shown in assembly diagram, *below,* to secure.

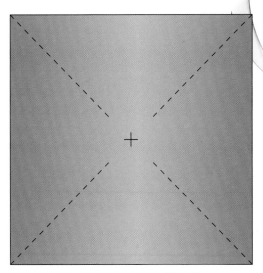

PINWHEEL MARKING DIAGRAM

ASSEMBLY DIAGRAM

Trinket Tins

Adorned with cheerful clay flowers, polka dots, and decorative banding, these little tins are just the right size for organizing in the kitchen or office.

what you'll need
Small tins (available in crafts stores or as spice tins in discount stores)
Oven-bake clay, such as Sculpey
Cookie sheet
Paper clip
Large seed beads
Rolling pin
Ruler; crafts knife
Scallop-edge scissors
Strong clear adhesive, such as Liquid Nails

here's how

1 For each tin, form a small clay flower to fit the lid. Roll small balls or ovals as petals, or roll a long rope and coil it. Add a desired center to each flower. Place flowers on a cookie sheet.

2 To make leaves, roll a small ball. Flatten it slightly and shape into a leaf. Flatten again if necessary. Add to clay flower.

3 To add indentations, use a paper clip. Use the rounded end to add vein lines or the tip of a paper clip to add small holes.

4 To add polka dots to the tin base, make pea-size balls from clay. Place on cookie sheet. Press a seed bead in the center of each piece of clay.

5 To add a dotted band to the tin base, roll out a piece of clay until it is approximately ⅛-inch thick. Use a ruler and a crafts knife to cut one straight edge. Carefully lift clay up and cut a scalloped edge ½ inch from the straight edge. Place around tin base, positioning low enough to avoid interfering with the placement of the lid. Press a seed bead into the clay by every other scallop.

6 To add a twisted rope trim to the tin base, choose two colors of clay. Roll each into thin ropes. Twist the ropes together. Place twisted rope around the tin base as desired. Cut away excess clay. Press seed beads into clay where desired.

7 Bake the clay pieces in the oven according to the manufacturer's instructions. Let cool.

8 Glue the clay pieces on the tins. Let the glue dry.

Butterfly Box

Everyone would welcome a box for organizing—especially one that is as delightful as this! Trimmed with scrapbook papers, decorative eyelets, and a clay butterfly, this charming box will never get lost among the clutter.

what you'll need

Small photo storage box in solid color
Scrapbook papers to coordinate with box
Crafts knife
Ruler
Glue stick
Floral stickers or decorative scrapbooking
  photo corners
Decorative eyelets, such as flowers and hearts
  (available in scrapbooking stores)
Paper punch
Eyelet tool
Clay in black and green or other desired color
Wire in black or other dark color
Hot-glue gun and hot-glue sticks

here's how

1 Using the box lid as a guide, cut the papers to fit the lid top as shown, *opposite*. Glue the papers together using a glue stick. Glue the papers on the lid. Add a sticker to each corner.

2 To add eyelets on the lid sides, measure and make a mark every ½ inch. Use a paper punch to make a hole over each mark. Using an eyelet tool, add an eyelet to every hole.

3 To make butterfly, form two marble-size clay balls and two slightly larger balls. Flatten each ball. Press the edges of the two large clay balls together to make the wing tops. Press the edges of the two small clay balls together for the wing bottoms. Press the tops and bottoms together. Roll a marble-size ball from black clay. Shape into a rope for the butterfly body. Press into place.

4 Fold the wire in half. Shape each end into a coil. Press the antennae into the top of the butterfly's head. Press eyelets into wings to make dots. Place the butterfly on a cookie sheet and place in the oven. Bake according to the manufacturer's directions. Let cool.

5 Hot-glue the butterfly to the center of the box lid. Add two or three floral stickers by the butterfly.

Dazzling Desk Set

These paint-splashed accessories
are sure to garner smiles.
Choose bright colors to liven up
a black desk set or pastel shades to
enhance off-white pieces.

what you'll need

Rubbing alcohol
Desk set in black or off-white
Acrylic enamel paints in pink, green, blue,
  and white
Disposable plate; paintbrush

here's how

1 Clean the surfaces of the desk set with rubbing alcohol. Let dry.

2 Put a small amount of each paint color on the plate. Add a drop or two of white to each color without mixing. When using paint, pick up the color and a little white on the paintbrush. Brush once lightly on the plate to slightly blend the colors.

3 Paint simple playful motifs, such as squares, circles, and stripes, on the black or off-white plastic areas of the desk set. Wash the brush before changing colors. Let the paint dry.

Fruits and Flowers

Spread some old-fashioned birthday cheer. Present this colorful fruit-studded spread inside a sugar bowl made beautiful with a hand-painted flower motif.

what you'll need for the jar

Sugar bowl with raised or recessed design
Glass paints in desired colors
Fine-line paintbrush

here's how

1 Wash and dry the bowl and lid. Avoid touching the areas to be painted.

2 Use paints and a paintbrush to enhance the bowl's established design. Use as many or as few colors as you desire. To make tiny dots, dip the handle of a paintbrush into paint and dot onto the bowl. Let the paint dry.

3 Bake the painted glassware in the oven if instructed by the paint manufacturer. Let cool.

what you'll need for the almond-raisin butter

½	cup golden raisins
2	tablespoons orange juice
2	tablespoons sliced almonds, toasted
½	cup butter or margarine, softened
1½	teaspoons finely shredded orange peel (set aside)

Note: Choose the fruit to match the colors you paint on the sugar bowl. Dried cranberries, dried blueberries, and dried tart red cherries all make excellent substitutes for the raisins. The spread tastes great on toast or pancakes.

here's how

1 In a blender container or food processor bowl, combine raisins and orange juice. Cover and blend or process with several on-off turns (avoid grinding). Add almonds; cover and blend or process with several on-off turns until chopped. Set aside.

2 In a medium mixing bowl beat butter with an electric mixer on medium speed until light and fluffy. Add raisin mixture and orange peel; stir until combined. Cover and store in the refrigerator for up to one week. Serve at room temperature. Makes 1 cup.

Take-Out Temptations

Tuck these airy macaroons into a take-out box that shouts "Happy Birthday" with its streamer and confetti stickers.

what you'll need for container

Stickers in desired shapes and colors
Plastic Chinese food container (available in paper supply stores)
Tissue paper
Noisemaker
Curling ribbon
Scissors

here's how

1 First decide on the arrangement of the stickers. Apply stickers to the sides of the container. Line box with tissue paper and fill with macaroons.

2 Tie noisemaker to container's handle using a ribbon. To curl ribbon, carefully pull ribbon across a scissor blade.

what you'll need for hickory nut macaroons

- 4 egg whites
- 4 cups sifted powdered sugar
- 2 cups chopped hickory nuts, black walnuts, or toasted pecans

here's how

1 In a large mixing bowl beat egg whites with an electric mixer on high speed until stiff, but not dry, peaks form. Gradually add powdered sugar, about ¼ cup at a time, beating at medium speed just until combined. Then beat 1 to 2 minutes more or until well combined. Fold in the nuts by hand.

2 Drop mixture by rounded teaspoons 2 inches apart onto cookie sheets lined with parchment paper or greased foil.

3 Bake in a 325°F oven about 15 minutes or until edges are very light brown.* Transfer cookies to wire racks and let cool. Store in a tightly covered container at room temperature for up to three days or in the freezer for up to three months. Makes 36 cookies.

*Note: It is normal for these cookies to split around the edges as they bake.

Sunrise Surprise

For a gift that really rises and shines, wrap a container in decorative paper and fill it with homemade pancake mix.

what you'll need
for the container

Scissors; red decorative paper
Cylinder container with lid that holds 10 cups
Spray adhesive; gold art paper
Wheat stamp or desired design
Ink pad in desired color
Decorative paper scraps; paper punch; raffia

here's how

1 Cut red decorative paper so it wraps around container with the edges overlapping slightly. Trim excess paper. Lay decorative paper on flat work surface. Spray adhesive on back side of the paper. Apply paper to container.

2 To make stamped accent paper, tear a wide band from gold art paper to apply to the center of the container. Lay the paper, right side up, on a work surface. Load stamp with ink and press onto the paper as many times as desired, turning the stamp in various directions. Let ink dry. Turn the paper over and spray with adhesive. Apply paper to the center of container. Let dry.

3 Trace around lid on a piece of stamped paper. Cut out circle. Spray the back side with adhesive and affix to container lid. Let dry.

4 For the tag, cut and fold a small rectangular tag from decorative paper scraps. Punch a hole in one corner. Tie the gift tag onto the container using a strand of raffia. Include mix directions, *opposite*, with the gift.

what you'll need for the
buttermilk pancake mix

8   cups all-purpose flour
2   cups buttermilk powder
½   cup sugar
2   tablespoons plus 2 teaspoons
       baking powder
4   teaspoons baking soda
2   teaspoons salt

here's how

1 In a large mixing bowl combine flour, buttermilk powder, sugar, baking powder, baking soda, and salt. Stir until combined. Store in an airtight container in a cool, dry place for up to six weeks or in a freezer container in the freezer for up to six months. Makes about 10 cups.

152

Mix Directions

2 eggs, slightly beaten
1⅔ cups water
⅓ cup margarine or butter, melted, or cooking oil
2½ cups Buttermilk Pancake Mix

1 Combine eggs, water, and margarine. Add Buttermilk Pancake Mix. Stir just until combined but still slightly lumpy. Heat a lightly greased griddle or heavy skillet over medium heat until a few drops of water dance across the surface. For each pancake, pour ¼ cup batter onto hot griddle; spread into a 4-inch circle.

2 Cook over medium heat until pancakes are golden brown, turning to cook second sides when pancake surfaces are bubbly and edges are slightly dry (about 2 to 3 minutes per side). Serve immediately or keep warm in a loosely covered ovenproof dish in a 300°F oven. If desired, serve with a favorite syrup or topping. Makes 16 pancakes.

Brownie Surprise

A simple plastic food container makes a dandy dome and tray for this peanut butter-glazed, candy-topped brownie.

what you'll need for the dome container

7- to 8-inch round plastic food container

Paint pens in desired colors; ice pick

Birthday cake candleholders; birthday candles

here's how

1 Turn the bowl portion of the plastic container upside down. Use paint pens to make scallops or other desired designs on the bottom and sides of the container as if decorating a birthday cake. Let dry.

2 Use an ice pick to poke holes in a circle around the flat bottom of the container. Put the candleholders into the holes. Put birthday candles into the holders.

what you'll need for the brownie

¼ cup butter

2 ounces unsweetened chocolate, chopped

3 tablespoons creamy peanut butter

1 egg, beaten

¾ cup sugar

½ cup all-purpose flour

½ teaspoon vanilla

1 recipe Peanut Butter Glaze

⅓ cup assorted candies, chopped

here's how

1 Grease a 6-inch springform pan. Set aside. In a heavy small saucepan melt butter and chocolate over low heat, stirring frequently. Stir in peanut butter. Cool about 10 minutes. In a medium mixing bowl stir together the beaten egg, sugar, flour, and vanilla. Stir in the cooled chocolate mixture. Pour batter into the prepared pan.

2 Bake in a 350°F oven for 35 minutes. Cool for 10 minutes on a wire rack. Loosen sides of springform pan. Cool brownie completely.

3 Remove sides of springform pan and, using a thin metal spatula or knife, loosen bottom of brownie from bottom of pan. Carefully transfer brownie to a flat plate or a 7- or 8-inch cardboard round that's covered with foil.

4 Prepare Peanut Butter Glaze. Pour warm glaze over cooled brownie, spreading evenly and allowing it to drip down sides. Top with assorted candies. Store in a tightly covered container in the refrigerator for up to three days (or freeze unglazed brownie for up to one month). Makes 1 brownie.

Peanut Butter Glaze: In a heavy small saucepan melt 2 tablespoons creamy peanut butter and 1 tablespoon butter over low heat. Remove from heat and stir in ¾ cup sifted powdered sugar. Stir in 2 teaspoons very hot water. Stir in additional hot water, 1 teaspoon at a time, to desired consistency.

Jewel-Topped Coffee Mix

Presented in a jewel-topped shaker jar, this coffee mix gives
its recipients good reason to take a break during the busy holiday season.
And that's a rare gift indeed!

what you'll need for the jar

Shaker jar with ring lid
Decorative paper
Pencil
Scissors
Button
Wire cutters
Hot-glue gun and hot-glue sticks
Ribbons

here's how

1 Layer ingredients into shaker jar as directed in recipe. Trace around the lid onto decorative paper. Cut out slightly smaller than traced line. Place paper on lid, under the ring. Adjust lid on top of jar. If necessary, cut off the shank of the button using wire cutters. Hot-glue the button in the center of the paper circle. Let it dry. Tie ribbons around the lid. Include mix directions, *right*, with gift.

what you'll need for the café au lait mix

½   cup powdered nondairy creamer
½   cup buttermints, lightly crushed
¼   cup sifted powdered sugar
2   cups nonfat dry milk powder
⅔   cup instant coffee crystals
    Peppermint sticks or round hard candies
    (optional)

here's how

1 In a medium mixing bowl stir together nondairy creamer, buttermints, powdered sugar, and milk powder. Layer mixture with coffee crystals, dividing among two 2-cup jars. If desired, insert peppermint sticks or candies to fill jars snugly. Cover and store in a cool, dry place for up to six weeks. Makes 2 cups of each layer, enough to fill two jars.

Mix Directions

1 For each serving, place ¼ cup of the mix in a mug and add ⅔ cup boiling water. Stir until the mix dissolves. Serve with a peppermint stick or candy if desired.

Index

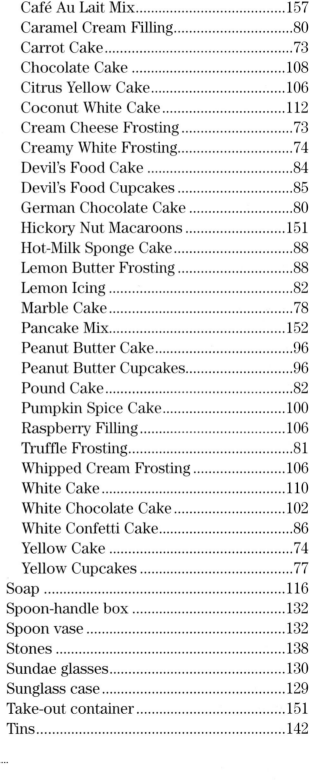

Credits & Sources

Designers

Susan M. Banker—Pages 10, 12, 22, 26, 59, 117, 120, 129, 130, 131, 135, 142, 144, 146, and 148.

Heidi Boyd—Page 126.

Donna Chesnut—Pages 128 and 131.

Carol Dahlstrom—Pages 11, 20, 50, 116, 138, and 140.

Phyllis Dunstan—Pages 119, 124, 125, 133, 134, 150, and 154.

Kathy Moenkhaus—Pages 47, 53, and 122–123.

Alice Wetzel—Pages 9, 15, 16, 18, 25, 30, 32, 34, 35, 37, 38, 41, 43, 44, 46, 48, 51, 54, 56, 60, 139, 153, and 156.

Cake Designer

Jennifer Petersen

Photographers

Andy Lyons Cameraworks
Bill Hopkins
Peter Krumhardt
Scott Little

Photostyling

Carol Dahlstrom
Donna Chesnut, assistant

Products

Beads
Gay Bowles Sales/Mill Hill
P.O. Box 1060
Janesville, WI 53547
www.millhill.com
1-800–356–9438

Cake supplies
Wilton Industries
1-800-794-5866
www.wilton.com

Notions
Prym-Dritz Corporation
P.O. Box 5028
Spartanburg, SC 29304

Ribbon
CM Offray & Son Inc.
Route 24, Box 601
Chester, NJ 07930-0601
1-908–879–4700

If you enjoyed this book, look for these other inspiring titles.